Transform Your Supply Chain

To Ken Bowers: Friend and Mentor

and, as ever,
Jack, Claire and Linda

■ SMART STRATEGIES SERIES ■

Transform Your Supply Chain

Releasing Value in Business

Jon Hughes

Mark Ralf

Bill Michels

INTERNATIONAL THOMSON BUSINESS PRESS

I(T)P ® An International Thomson Publishing Company

London ● Bonn ● Boston ● Johannesburg ● Madrid ● Melbourne ● Mexico City ● New York ● Paris
Singapore ● Tokyo ● Toronto ● Albany, NY ● Belmont, CA ● Cincinnati, OH ● Detroit, MI

Transform Your Supply Chain: Releasing Value in Business

Copyright © 1998 Jon Hughes, Mark Ralf and Bill Michels

First published by International Thomson Business Press

   A division of International Thomson Publishing Inc.
The ITP logo is a trademark under licence

British Library Cataloguing-in-Publication Data
A catalogue record for this book is available from the British Library.

Library of Congress Catalog-in-Publication Data
A catalog record for this book is available from the Library of Congress.

First edition 1998

Typeset by the Windsor Foundation for Business Development, Mark Ralf and Wild Associates. Printed in the UK by TJ International, Padstow, Cornwall.

ISBN 1-86152-054-9

International Thomson Business Press
Berkshire House
168-173 High Holborn
London WC1V 7AA
UK

International Thomson Business Press
20 Park Plaza
13th Floor
Boston MA 02116
USA

http:\\www.itbp.com

Contents

List of figures

List of cases

Preface and acknowledgements

This is a book written primarily for business executives. Over recent years a number of excellent publications have emerged which examine the supply chain from an academic or theoretical perspective. These have made a necessary and important contribution to the development of thinking on the subject. But they have not always addressed the vital areas of business growth, bottom line profitability and the creation of shareholder value in terms that can be readily embraced by senior managers and functional leaders. Influencing their thinking requires a more direct coverage of practical interventions capable of transforming the supply chain. This book addresses that need. In addition, it has been structured to facilitate ready access to core themes and key messages through extensive use of icons, graphics, charts and case studies. We hope that this will make the reading more enjoyable.

The authors have spent a considerable part of the past two decades in developing and applying the strategies detailed in this book with companies and clients in over thirty countries worldwide. It has been our privilege to work alongside a considerable number of influential executives, change drivers and avid professionals. We would like to acknowledge their contribution to the development of our own thinking. While the list is long, the following stand out for their fortitude, friendship and preparedness to apply often emergent ideas within their own organisations: Chuck Adams, Euan Blackwood, Phil Boyd, Barry Brenner, Tony Coffey, Robin Cammish, J.J. Carr, Larry Davis, Philippa Dickson, Robin Forrester, Louis G. Greis, Narotam Kumar Gupta, Clive Heal, Ray Jones, Edward M. Lewis, Michael J. McMullen, Jagan Mallya, David Malpiedi, Joe Meier, Edward Monsour, Mike Nelson, Robert Nelson, Owen Parmenter, Simon Pau, the late James E. Petty, William Petty, Vernon Sankey, John M. Scales, Edward A. Schefer, Herb Schmidt, Michael Starks, Iain Stewart, Liam Strong, the late Alan Thynne, Bill Walsh, Martin Ward, Julie Woodin and Stephen Wright.

We were fortunate indeed in being able to draw on the depth of expertise that exists within the Windsor Foundation for Business Development, ADR International Purchasing Consultants and our design consultancy, Wild Associates in Cheam, Surrey. Noteworthy contributions were made by Ian Billson, Mark Goodman, Hight Harrison, David Hughes, John Matthews, Kevin Wild, Giles Wright and, especially, Jacqueline Cottew. Without her encouragement, commitment and tireless endeavour the manuscript would have remained as no more than an interesting concept and loose collection of abstracts.

Also, throughout the writing process, Claire Ralf and Linda Michels provided their usual help and encouragement and one of the team would also like to acknowledge David and Stephen Ralf for being the best of distractions.

A common denominator across the authoring team is their commitment to active networking and open sharing of business concepts through conferences and workshops as well as collaboration with a number of universities and educational centres worldwide. As a result, a strong relationship has developed with the Centre for Strategy and Procurement Management at the University of Birmingham. We wish to acknowledge the friendship and intellectual leadership of Andrew Cox and the core CSPM team of Paul Ireland, Chris Lonsdale, Joe Sanderson, Ian Thompson and Glyn Watson. Their research and publications in the years ahead will be well worth reading.

Finally, we wish to thank the staff of International Thomson Business Press in London for their tolerance and professionalism as they allowed us to restructure their publishing supply chain. The input, guidance and active support of Julian Thomas, Penny Grose and So-Shan Au have been warmly appreciated. When planning the project we could not have expected to locate such a receptive and professional team.

Clearly, there are also many other colleagues, clients and collaborators who have influenced us over the years. To this 'unacknowledged majority' please accept a sincere thank you for all your support. We wish you, and the readers of this book, the best of future success in transforming your supply chains.

Jon Hughes	*Mark Ralf*	*Bill Michels*
Windsor,	Cheam,	Ann Arbor,
England.	England.	U.S.A.

CHAPTER ONE

Reversing neglect: Releasing the value

Dominate or die: achieving pre-eminence in the market

Creating, understanding, impacting, managing, serving, manipulating and exploiting markets are the common denominators of corporate strategy and business development. Benign, progressive, collaborative and beneficial interventions for shareholders, stakeholders and society alike, may co-exist with a darker side of collusion, opportunism, fear, greed and contempt for so-called trading partners. This is the reality of business, and one that provides the context for any serious attempt to transform the supply chain, either in its entirety or on a piecemeal basis. Both perspectives, and the complexities of their dynamics and interaction, will be fully addressed within this book.

Indeed, as a commentator on business, it is easy to fall into the trap of describing and offering a sanitized, homogenized view of the drivers behind many of the business strategies possible within markets. While the supply chain provides a most useful model for the planning and delivery of initiatives in efficiency maximization and

'A healthy bottom line begins with the top line. The sustainable health of a business depends on recurring top–line growth.'
Richard Brown, CEO, Cable & Wireless.

1

process optimization these are essentially operational improvement strategies. There is significantly greater conceptual and strategic power to be gained by adopting a supply chain perspective that focuses in a proactive manner on to vigorous market management, customer development and business growth. Figure 1.1, and the model it represents, is no more than a simple and stylistic representation of conventional supply chain thinking, wherein a number of stages or links exist in a supply process from primary manufacture or creation of a service through to its delivery to an end customer or consumer. This emphasizes an integrative approach and implies the need for optimization and co-ordination. That is only part of the story. As will be seen throughout this book, the strategic, operational and change management options that are available to companies are much more extensive and complex in practice. Because so few organizations have really approached the supply chain in such a comprehensive and searching manner, there are enormous opportunities to create and release additional value for both shareholders and stakeholders. The level of past neglect determines the size of the opportunity.

Impacting top line and bottom line

Maximizing profit, or the excess of current revenues over costs, is the fundamental driver and motivator for business activity and executive decision making. This enables management to meet their obligations to owners or shareholders in terms of increased earnings. Clearly, decisions may be taken in the short term to forgo current profits and concentrate on market penetration, volume growth, restructuring the organization, and new product development. But any successful business will return as speedily as possible to its primary goal of building profit through simultaneously maximizing revenues while minimizing costs.

A concerted focus on to the interventions necessary to create industry, sector or niche leadership is one of the foremost strategies being applied to achieve this goal. Securing and sustaining a dominant or pre-eminent position, while remaining intensely focused and responsive to customer needs, should be the preoccupation of any business development strategy.   This usually enables a company to raise or, at worst, maintain prices ahead of costs without losing market share. While this can be achieved through the effective operational implementation of carefully framed strategic intent, the definition and direction of market management strategies are much more

'You cannot shrink to greatness.' Edward E. Lawler, Professor in Organizational Behaviour, University of Southern California.

Figure 1.1

The supply chain assumes a flow of value to the customer and pricing pressure to the supplier. Reality is a lot more complex

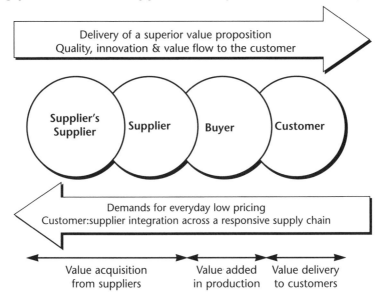

important than purely operational effectiveness.   This is why in Figure 1.2 overleaf, it is essential to consider carefully the different types of supply chains that can be identified (and the listing is not exhaustive), and then assess their contribution to these two different approaches. From a business growth standpoint, the key is to create, as far as possible, a unique and sustainable competitive position.

Figure 1.2

Nine types of supply chain can be identified across a wide range of sectors. Each meets different types of business need

1. Arm's length, open competition

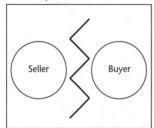

Competitive bids, tenders and market testing.
Emphasize rigour and tough bargaining.

2. Commodity trading: A sells to B sells to C sells to A

Independent trading driven by the deal.
Emphasize the need to manage volatility with commodities.

3. Partnering for customer delight

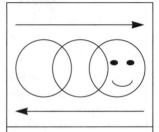

Openness, trust and shared deliverables.
Emphasize performance upstream & value downstream.

4. From suppliers' suppliers to customers' customers

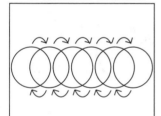

Link up all the players in a horizontal supply chain.
Emphasize seamless delivery, optimization and integration.

5. Lean supply chains and systems integration

War on waste and step change cost transformation.
Emphasize lean as in fit, not lean as in starving.

6. Competing constellations of linked companies

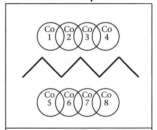

First movers link up with the best players.
Emphasize capability, competence and cultural compatibility.

7. Interlocking network supply between competitors

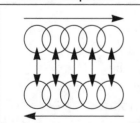

Link up for incremental business.
Emphasize an association where little competitive advantage.

8. Asset control supply: dominate or die

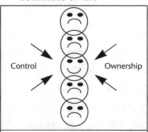

Gain control of the assets and leverage them.
Emphasize staying the right side of monopoly abuse.

9. Virtual supply. No production, only customers

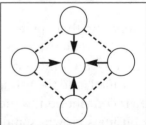

Low fixed costs and sub-contract production.
Emphasize marketing skills and superb distribution.

A number of searching questions about the market and your ability to develop it can then be raised in the context of business growth and profit maximization.

- What are the truly distinctive and genuinely sustainable capabilities of your business, and how do they need to change in the future?
- Where are the most appropriate markets in which to apply them?
- Do you intend to focus on current markets or new ones?
- Is it possible to redraw the market boundaries or reframe the rules of engagement?
- Where are the new sources of revenue generation, and what types of products are required to tap them?
- Is maximum differentiation on your products to be achieved through innovation, new product development, control of critical technologies, or service levels?
- Should the emphasis be on a complete product or the creation of a key module for use or sale by a third party?
- To what extent do you possess the resources and capital to exploit these opportunities alone?
- Is there a need to form alliances, joint ventures or networks with other companies to achieve this?
- Will these be permanent or temporary, offensive or defensive, and genuinely collaborative or exploitative?
- What are the implications for pricing, positioning and relationship management with customers, competitors and suppliers?
- To what extent do your relationships with third parties support or dilute your efforts?
- How can reputation be built and sustained through customer responsiveness and emotional appeal?
- Will supply lines undermine or damage this reputation?

'Within historical cycles, there has not been a single industry that has continued to be prosperous for 40 to 60 years.' Hiroshi Okuda, President, Toyota Motor, on the need to increase its non-vehicle business capabilities through alliances and joint ventures.

Power, pre-eminence and profitability

It should be readily apparent that both power and profit margin accrue to those companies which possess some form of indispensability within the supply chain. This can be attained through first mover advantages secured through close analysis of the market and customer needs, superior product development, exemplary service offerings, the construction of entry barriers or the control and ownership of strategic capabilities and essential technologies at crucial points in the chain.

Dominance, pre-eminence and indispensability through the application of such strategies, and their ready conversion into highly profitable revenue streams, may generate superior returns for owners, employees and share-holders. Such legitimate profits are justified for successful strategic endeavour. But the precise market interventions, and the nature of their exploitation, can also become an ethical issue. At several points in this book the subject of market domination and collusive behaviour will be addressed. As an illustration, the case study in Figure 1.3, drawn from the supply chain for soft drinks in the USA, demonstrates the ways in which profit margin secured by the various parties can only be understood within the context of complex market dynamics, available capacity, volume throughputs and efficiencies, control of technolo-gies, government regulation and the preparedness of companies to collude and leverage their power against the interests of the end customer or consumer. Anyone with significant experience of a range of business sectors will readily appreciate the accuracy of that statement.

Understanding the true nature of business relation-ships, and how they impact both companies and their customers, is a most important element in active manage-ment of the supply chain. It receives significant attention within this book. There are clearly many different relational types available, and they are capable of delivering both beneficial and negative outcomes. Their active evalu-ation, creation and management is a crucial competence.

Avoiding the trade-offs of cost and differentiation

Conventional business development models over the past two decades have emphasized that companies should choose and then implement a clearly defined strategy

Figure 1.3

Supply chains are not just a series of links to be integrated. Recognize that power, processes and profitability have to be addressed

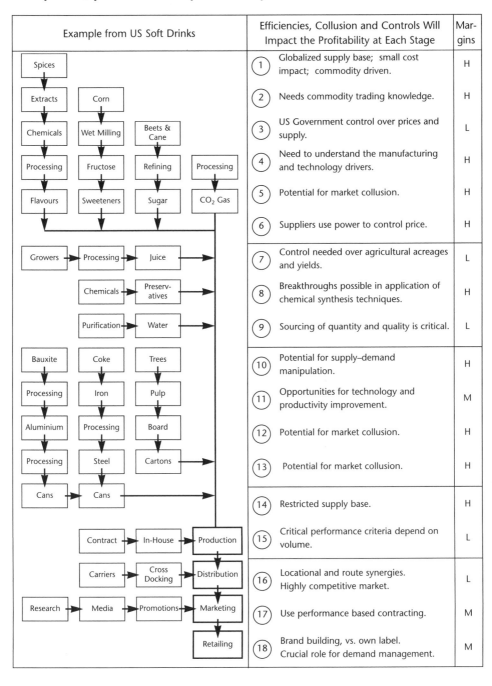

Example from US Soft Drinks	Efficiencies, Collusion and Controls Will Impact the Profitability at Each Stage	Margins
	1 Globalized supply base; small cost impact; commodity driven.	H
	2 Needs commodity trading knowledge.	H
	3 US Government control over prices and supply.	L
	4 Need to understand the manufacturing and technology drivers.	H
	5 Potential for market collusion.	H
	6 Suppliers use power to control price.	H
	7 Control needed over agricultural acreages and yields.	L
	8 Breakthroughs possible in application of chemical synthesis techniques.	H
	9 Sourcing of quantity and quality is critical.	L
	10 Potential for supply–demand manipulation.	H
	11 Opportunities for technology and productivity improvement.	M
	12 Potential for market collusion.	H
	13 Potential for market collusion.	H
	14 Restricted supply base.	H
	15 Critical performance criteria depend on volume.	L
	16 Locational and route synergies. Highly competitive market.	L
	17 Use performance based contracting.	M
	18 Brand building, vs. own label. Crucial role for demand management.	M

Avoid single prescriptions. Real sustainable advantage is delivered from the way in which a number of activities fit together within a unique strategic and operational framework. Different firms need different pathways to success. Strategic capability is about creating, evaluating and selecting the most appropriate options.

which is based either on cost leadership (producing goods and services at the lowest cost relative to competitors), or alternatively a strategy of differentiation (where goods or services possess special attributes or functionality that justify premium price). The arguments for this focused approach have encouraged companies to compete principally through the attainment of a cost advantage or via the supply of some valued point of competitor differentiation such as quality or customer service. Such a strategic trade-off is no longer appropriate. Throughout this book there will be many illustrations of companies which either have secured or are striving to attain both lowest cost and the highest product or service quality. This is well illustrated by the Dell case study.

As can be seen in Figure 1.4, however, building superior internal organizational capability, an external network of committed and motivated suppliers and properly responsive distribution channels requires very

Figure 1.4

Transforming the supply chain requires explicit definition and evaluation of a number of preferred strategic options

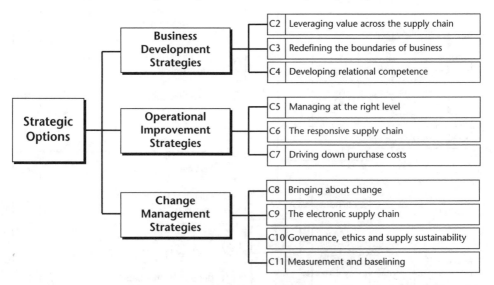

Each transformational option is examined, chapter by chapter, within this book. They are also drawn together within an audit tool for use by senior management. This can be found in the Appendix.

Case Study:

Dell Computer Corporation

Focus and positioning: using the supply chain for business advantage

Dell is the second largest supplier of desktop PCs to the corporate market. Sales growth is increasing at 40% per annum, twice the rate for the sector. With $10 billion revenue they rank fifth behind Compaq, IBM, Apple and NEC.

As the case study byline adapted from founder and CEO Michael Dell suggests, business success is simple. Simplify your supply chain; sell direct to the customer; cut out the dealers; build to customer requirements; make to order.

And yet, in the early 1990s, Dell was beset by cash flow problems. Their internal organizational competencies and supply capabilities could not deal with volume growth and inevitable manufacturing complexities. Poor production and costly errors had caused multi-million write-offs and re-tooling. Off-strategy retailer partnerships had failed. So what business practices have led to the bounce back?

1. **Maintain and extend the prime focus on the corporate customer**. Seek their views. Encourage them to influence technology. Respond vigorously to their needs. (For example, every year Dell runs a two day breakout retreat with the senior executives of all major customers.)

2. **Bypass the distributors and dealers**.

This does not just cut costs and secure margin. It allows Dell to keep in close touch with customer reactions and trends. They face the real external market rather than accepting retrospective review from third party market research.

3. **Align production to future trends**. Dell holds just over two weeks' inventory compared to 48 days for Compaq. The norm in the sector is well in excess of 60 days. Stock is turned over 30+ times a year. With figures like this, gross margins and return on capital are high: 21% and 106% respectively.

4. **Adopt responsive supply**. Low stocks, fast turnaround and strongly customer focused distribution networks are key elements in Dell's supply. In a sector where obsolescence and price competition rapidly force down memory and processor chip prices, you need to avoid being left with expensive old stock.

5. **Close supply chain collaboration.** Alignment with Intel and Microsoft has paid off. Co-marketing and pre-loaded software tap into the vast market of potential home users.

6. **Make purchasing easy**. Dell secures sales via the Internet and corporate intranets.

In too many strategy texts there is no mention of people. There is an absence of an employee perspective and the available options in change management. Democratize strategy. Engage considerable numbers of your staff in its creation and delivery. The minimum number of change agents is the square root of the total employed.

significant executive focus over a number of years to determine the appropriate allocation of capital and resources between business development strategies and operational improvement initiatives.

Strategy, of course, is nothing without implementation. Resistance to change, and failure to involve a critical mass of staff in the process, can undermine the most carefully crafted programme of innovation. While we advocate a structured approach to supply chain transformation, as shown in Figure 1.5, it is not implied that strategic action and operational improvement are necessarily based on linear thinking and ways of working. It is an iterative process of joint development between the organization, its staff and closely involved suppliers and third parties. This perspective will be emphasized throughout the book.

Figure 1.5

A structured approach to supply chain transformation facilitates business development and operational improvement

Gather the Data
- Internal assessment of current approaches to the supply chain
- External analysis of marketplace trends and customer opportunities

Challenge the Thinking
- Formation of a supply chain strategy forum to assess the needs
- Cascade of executive-led project groups to scrutinize core processes

Frame the Strategies
- Definition of required target returns and release of shareholder value
- Development of supply chain strategies to achieve these goals

Implement the Change
- Allocation of business development strategies to sponsor executives
- Prioritization of operational improvement strategies and 'quick wins'

Measure the Outcome
- Integration of supply chain measurement in corporate wide reviews
- Baselining to maintain pressure for performance delivery

CHAPTER TWO

Leveraging value across the supply chain

Overview

1. Acquiring, delivering and appropriating value
2. Creating a customer responsive strategy
3. Power, pre-eminence and dominance
4. Building and protecting strategic capabilities
5. Balancing price and functionality
6. Leveraging knowledge to create and deliver value
7. The implications of knowledge management
8. Fear, greed and desire in commodity markets
9. The market victim
10. Breaking traditional cycles of influence

The Bottom Line

Business success results from superior performance of a product, sold at the most leveraged price, with extraordinary levels of service and compelling emotional values. This cannot occur without thoroughly understanding the value proposition and the nature of power in markets.

Acquiring, delivering and appropriating value

Executives across a broad spectrum of market sectors are striving to adapt to accelerating competition, the consequences of shorter product life cycles, rapid commoditization of once differentiated products and a corresponding weakness in overall pricing across many categories. There is a growing appreciation that the competitive landscape is changing. Past strategies and operational initiatives appear to be losing their impact. Not surprisingly, therefore, companies are looking for new sources of business advantage. Throughout this chapter, nine core themes will be emphasized to demonstrate the role of the supply chain in providing such an advantage:

- align the whole of your business to the delivery of profitable, compelling, superior customer value;
- recognize that it is through the knowledge and capabilities of both your staff *and* the other parties in the supply chain that you achieve this goal;
- only a fraction of this knowledge and capability is being deployed appropriately and is a prime target for renewal, development and leveraging;
- value needs to be delivered to customers in a way that sustains profitability of the business while meeting fully the expectations of shareholders;
- achieving this return requires the appropriation of value for shareholders;
- securing a pre-eminent or dominant position in the market place facilitates such appropriation;
- dominance can come from the superiority of the product offering, its pricing, striking differentiation, control of capabilities and the ability to exercise power and influence over each of the stages of supply;
- defining appropriate value requires a detailed understanding of the relationship between the price and functionality of products and services;
- the total organization needs to be aligned in this way.

Understanding the nature of value

Despite the apparently obvious advantages of focusing on delivering superior value to customers, it can be surprising how many companies manage to avoid and evade this prime executive task. It can be seen from Figure 2.1 that there are a number of options available. Model A is inappropriate. Model B majors on customer needs and is the central message of this chapter. Model C recognizes that power, privileged access to resources, dominance and even manipulation are also important drivers in the supply chain.

'The concept of mass marketing is less useful these days. People need to feel that the offer has been tailored individually to their needs.' Terry Leahy, CEO, Tesco.

All companies provide customers with an amount of value. This is a combination of the functionality of a product or service in terms of the benefits that are offered to the customer and the price that is charged. Clearly, to be successful, any venture must create value for which a customer is prepared to pay. Business success is secured

Figure 2.1

It is inappropriate to evaluate business strategies only via 'customer delight'. There is a shareholder and customer trade-off

Model A: Inwardly Focused: Product or Technology Led Strategy

Create a Product	Make the Product	Sell the Product
'This could be a great product.'	'How do we make it?'	'So, where are the customers?'

Model B: Customer Focused: Value Delivery and Customer Responsive Strategy

Define the Value	Provide the Value	Communicate the Value
'What are customers looking for?'	'Are price and functionality right?'	'How do we promote it?'

Model C: Shareholder Focused: Value Appropriation Strategy

Define the Returns	Dominate the Market	Supply the Product
'What's in the interests of shareholders?'	'How do we dominate the market?'	'How do we avoid antagonizing customers?'

'What do you do when your competitor is drowning? Get a live hose and stick it in his mouth.' Douglas Ivester, CEO and Chairman of Coca-Cola on the ruthless pursuit of dominance.

'Their Achilles' heel is their own arrogance, and it eventually will be their downfall. I hope I'm around to see it.' Craig Weatherup, Pepsi Global Beverage.

when superior value is delivered to a critical mass of customers at a high enough price over cost that the company achieves superior profitability, sustained growth and the creation of sufficient capital to invest in its future strategic capabilities. It must achieve this while fully protecting and leveraging these capabilities ahead of competitors. The Coca-Cola case study is a superb example.

Value equals benefits minus price. Clearly customers will select the product or service which they believe provides the superior value compared to competing alternatives. Business growth reflects the perceptions of customers that the product or service is of superior value. It is a fundamental requirement of a successful business, therefore, to choose a winning value proposition and then align all of its functions, processes, staff and suppliers to delivering it profitably.

Case Study:

Coca-Cola

Dominating the market for soft drinks through marketing and distribution

Coca-Cola's phenomenal success stems from its conviction that there is no mature market on the planet for its product. Potential demand is still huge.

It's easy to assume that this is hype and overstatement. After all, they sell almost a third of a trillion bottles of Coke, Diet Coke, Fanta and Sprite each year. That is 48% of the world soft drink market. They even outsell the leading tea in Britain, the leading bottled water in France and the leading coffee in Brazil. But they still have less than 3% of the total liquid intake world market. Their view is 'we are just getting started'.

Managing the distribution supply chain is one of the keys to current and future success. Its bottling partners, the companies that buy soft drink concentrate from Coca-Cola and mix it with water before bottling or canning it for local markets, are crucial links in the chain. 'Anchor' bottlers are used on a regional basis. These are the companies with the financial resources and management capabilities to match their ambitious growth targets. Coca-Cola owns equity shares in each of them, and has invested enormously in its soft drinks infrastructure. This allows top management to focus on global branding and market innovation.

Balancing price and functionality in value delivery

An absolutely crucial feature of business success is the ability to position products or services within the market place in a way that generates an acceptable and sustainable profit margin. This calls for full recognition of the impact on, and relationship between, the prices that customers are prepared to support and the level of appropriate functionality that is being provided by the product or service in meeting their needs.

It is this price-functionality linkage which defines value delivery and the specific business initiatives that are required to secure the maximum possible return from product and service development strategies. The relationship between pricing (and the way in which underlying costs are managed) and functionality (and associated product positioning in terms of a rigorous definition of customer needs) is crucial. Furthermore, it explains the likelihood of a company being able to maintain high levels of profitability, the probability of competitive attack from other companies and the linkage with necessary operational improvement strategies such as target costing (which is examined in more detail in Chapter Seven). Figure 2.2, overleaf, provides a useful summary of a number of the potential options available in the context of product design, development and market positioning.

In quadrant one, a new product is being offered at a low price and with low levels of functionality. Unless there is some form of regulatory protection or complete absence of competition, the product is either doomed or most unlikely to generate an acceptable return. It has probably been supplied either as the result of inferior decision making within the product development process, or because it is a readily available, non-differentiated commodity. However, it may still be able to generate high volumes, by virtue of being a new product or one where there is high natural demand, even though functionality is low. While it may deter competition, by virtue of the low price, it may

'Once you have
created a market, you
are faced with the
necessity of re-creating
it continually.' William
Olsten, CEO, Olsten
Corporation.

equally be capable of drawing in other companies if high volume accrues to the product. However, there is likely to be little prospect of generating higher prices, nor of building margin, in the future. Even if greater functionality were introduced, a number of competitors are likely to have entered the market. They will usually pursue copycat, 'me too' strategies and compete head-on with whatever additional features of functionality are offered to the customer.

Figure 2.2

Globally the commoditization of products, sectors and markets is accelerating. Differentiation, innovation and cost leadership are crucial

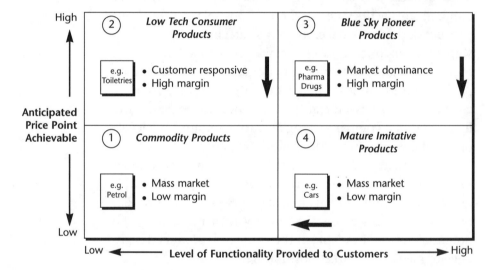

© ADR International Purchasing Consultants.

Quadrant two describes a volatile, high risk but potentially high reward market place. It characterizes many markets that respond quickly and positively to brand marketing. Hewlett-Packard's approach is typical. When a company adopts this strategy in the positioning and roll-out of new product launches, it needs to build or capture as much volume as possible before competitors enter the market in order to maximize the return on product development, marketing, distribution and other associated costs.

Case Study:
Hewlett-Packard
Balancing price and functionality in a winning value proposition

Hewlett-Packard is famous for its guiding principles. These are enshrined in 'the H.P. Way'. Empowerment, entrepreneurship, decentralized decision making and individual accountability are the mantras that trip off the HP executive tongue. So why, in their inkjet printer business, did they decide to change their whole way of working? Particularly since they had a market share of 50% plus, and were working flat out to meet demand.

This was because they decided that the real market for their product was the home consumer and not just the office worker. Defining the market, redeveloping the product and realigning the whole supply chain took just twelve months. They fundamentally changed their way of working to focus on this new customer.

1. Home consumers' purchasing patterns are much less predictable than the corporate market. This called for more flexible and responsive manufacturing. New plants were needed and brought on stream. Greater use was also made of contract manufacturers to smooth production during peak periods.

2. The corporate market was satisfied with purchasing from a range of just five Desk Jet models. Not so with home users. Over fifty product offerings had to be developed to cover copiers, fax, printers and scanners.

3. Such product proliferation drove up manufacturing and distribution complexity. But it was reduced by adopting common platforms.

4. In the past, factories had shipped complete finished goods to distribution centres and then on to dealers. A policy of postponement was adopted. Products were shipped in a generic state. Local features were then added for each specific market segment at the point of distribution.

5. The excellence of Hewlett-Packard's product was initially perceived negatively by customers. Quality was seen to be associated with an unjustifiable premium price. This perception was changed through more effective merchandising in store outlets and developing customer orientated relationships with the volume retailers.

6. Further functionality was added through product bundling deals with Microsoft and Walt Disney.

7. Sales staff in the past had been compensated on orders taken, rather than completed product sales. HP switched from push supply to a pull led demand system.

The Hewlett-Packard case example demonstrates the need for speed of response in both new product development and supply–demand integration.   Unfortunately for the developers of the product, if it gains favourable customer reaction it soon attracts 'me too' competitors. Prices can be forced down very quickly since the ability to compete through the addition of functionality is relatively easy. However, since functionality overall is quite low, a volume cap is often reached quite quickly. An appropriate strategy at this stage is the delivery of a planned programme of innovation which can increase functionality, and can also be used to support the next wave of marketing. The aim is then to differentiate the product at higher prices, and sustain the value relationship with the customer, until the pack of 'me too' competitors once again catches up. This cycle may be repeated many times over a number of years, and is typical of fast moving consumer goods in the household product, cleaning and toiletries sector. Innovation, new product development and the opportunities for supplier involvement in this process are covered in more detail in Chapter Three.

A third strategy, and in many ways the preferred one, is to develop new products which are launched with dramatically superior levels of functionality and in a manner that commands a high, premium price. These are the 'pioneer products' that may be so fundamentally different to anything currently available that they actually create a new market. This strategy can be hugely successful, but only if the levels of functionality can readily be sourced or manufactured and, most importantly, if the intellectual property rights relating to production and delivery can be protected. This is particularly true in the early days of the product, when it is essential to avert or inhibit the possibility of competitors entering the market, while building both volumes and customer loyalty to a commanding, dominant level. The ideal goal is for the innovator to be able to develop the market and, with some justification, reap the rewards of mass market volume, at a high price for this premium product.

There are three potential risks.   Firstly, that the premium price is pitched too high and damages sales volume. Secondly, that the premium pricing policy quickly draws in 'me too' competition. However, the high levels of functionality and control of intellectual property assets such as patents will usually block or, at worst, delay the onset of competition. Thirdly, the developer of the product may have little room for future price increases.   Since functionality is already high, improvements are likely to be at the margin. Certainly, as soon as 'me too' competition becomes established then further building of a price premium is most unlikely. Indeed, once that happens the product begins the inevitable downward spiral into maturity and eventual commoditization unless there is an injection of substantial innovation to raise the functionality to new heights.

There is, unfortunately, one further very serious operational risk within this third product positioning strategy. Pioneer products are often technology led. High functionality will have been the business driver. It is easy for this to be pursued without sufficiently prudent regard to cost. Because of the likelihood of the product achieving a premium price, a company can sometimes ignore the need for profitability to be designed into the product from concept creation onwards. This can be a blind spot for some businesses. Traditionally, this has been the major weakness of many technically excellent companies that have focused inwardly on their product development capabilities rather than their customer requirements. The case study on Knürr, from Germany's *Mittelstand*, is a typical example even though its products are not particularly innovative. Encouragingly, though, these deficiencies can be readily addressed through the application of the sorts of operational improvement strategies detailed in Chapters Six and Seven of this book. The key to success, as ever, is real commitment from top management to drive the internal and external changes needed to transform many fundamental processes within the supply chain.

An external focus on customer needs is the driver of effective value delivery. The internal organization is then aligned in a way that delivers this goal.

Finally, a fourth option is available for consideration; one which has particular relevance for product development in more mature markets. A strategy is applied whereby the product is launched at a low price but with high functionality. Target costing is adopted with all of the suppliers involved in its production. This ensures that satisfactory profitability will be achieved and it effectively acts as a barrier to 'me too' competitors unless they possess the

---

Case Study:
Knürr

Improving product offerings to customers while slashing manufacturing costs

Knürr is typical *Mittelstand*, the network of small to medium sized, often family owned businesses that fuel the German economy and its exports. It is a Munich based fabricator making cabinets and racks for customers in the electronics and instrumentation sector. Profitability in the early 1990s had crashed; its main market was in recession; there was insufficient focus on customer needs; and the cost base was unsustainable. So, how did it survive?

1. A major emphasis on new product development. Resource for design and marketing was increased. The customer base was redefined and broadened. Technical capabilities were leveraged. Innovative racks and cabinets for telecoms companies and hospitals were produced. These commanded higher prices with higher perceived functionality.

2. A big drive to reduce labour costs in manufacturing. A subsidiary was set up in the Czech Republic. 30% of components were outsourced to low-cost countries.

3. A readiness to be customer responsive. Speed, flexibility and adaptability became their hallmark. There was a complete review and redesign of their supply chain and manufacturing processes.

4. A challenge to internal business relationships. Integration and collaboration between designers, marketing staff, purchasing specialists and manufacturing professionals was emphasized.

5. The development of external alliances and licensing agreements in China, Singapore, Japan, India, Hungary and Brazil. These boosted exports and generated incremental profit through royalty payments.

By leveraging value and capability in this way, and being prepared to address both internal cultural issues as well as external relational opportunities, Knürr is once again profitable.

capabilities to match fully the mix of price, functionality and cost. Such a strategy is capable of stimulating rapid product take-up by customers and, in turn, ensuring that the cost drivers are contained further through scale benefits. This will simultaneously deter competitors from entering the market. However, such a strategy cannot be achieved by functionality alone. Rigorous application of target costing is essential to achieve the levels of perceived customer value on pricing that are needed to boost sales and achieve the necessary success in the market place.

Leveraging knowledge to create and deliver value

In many sectors, work is being transformed from the delivery of tangible products produced by manual labour, to the delivery of products and services created through the application and leveraging of knowledge and intellectual capability. The significance of knowledge based industries to the global economy as a whole can be seen by the rate at which knowledge is accumulating. For example, approximately 90% of everything known in the fields of biology, chemistry and physics has been discovered in the past thirty years. Indeed, it is estimated that knowledge is currently doubling every two years, and the pace is accelerating. Not surprisingly, therefore, there has been a major increase in knowledge based industries and professions. Since the early 1980s, the USA has experienced a 37% growth in managerial and professional occupations. In the UK, by 2000, it is estimated that there will be more than ten million knowledge workers, compared with only seven million manual workers.

> 'You need to know where the knowledge components reside so that you can bring them together in the service. Knowledge really is an asset. And treating it as such changes the lens through which you view the world.'
> Elisabeth Lank, Director of the Knowledge Programme, ICL.

Knowledge, however it is defined, is clearly a vital corporate capability. It is clearly a means of creating substantial value, although few organizations have the frameworks necessary for fully managing or measuring it. Indeed, there is a huge difference between the true value of knowledge and how companies are valued in published accounts and the stock market. One example will dramatically illustrate this situation. The top 500 companies in the Standard & Poor's Five Hundred Composite Stock Price Index, which accounts for approximately 70% of the value of all publicly traded US companies, had fixed assets of approximately $1.5 trillion at the end of 1996. But their combined stock value was a staggering $5 trillion. Even assuming that stock prices may be substantially overrated, intangible or knowledge based assets appear to represent a significant amount of the value gap between the market value of a company and its book value.

The implications of knowledge management

'Lots of the business relies on tacit knowledge. It is very hard to capture that.'
Marcus Spey, Director of Knowledge Management Services for Andersen Consulting.

The future profits of many organizations will increasingly be derived from intellectual capital rather than purely through production processes. The implications are that:

- companies need to acknowledge that they use only a small fraction of the knowledge that exists within their companies and across their supply chains;
- appropriate strategies are required to understand, measure, create, deploy, retain, transfer and protect knowledge;
- since there are relatively low fixed costs behind many knowledge based products and processes, rapid transfer of intellectual materials is possible;
- such transfer, and both its opportunities and risks, needs careful scrutiny. This is especially true since the 1990s has seen numerous waves of joint ventures, strategic alliances and collaborative agreements between companies. They are associated with massive flows of intellectual knowledge;
- an important distinction should be recognized between explicit knowledge, which is often found codified in the form of manuals and procedures, and tacit knowledge, which has been acquired by years of experience. The value of this knowledge is not always taken into account in downsizing and outsourcing initiatives.

Leveraging knowledge across the supply chain

Knowledge management has not yet been built into many of the models of business strategy and supply chain thinking. A pioneering exception can be seen in the case study. Skandia have created a systematic method for valuing and managing intellectual capital, which they have defined as the competence and capabilities of their employees, the company's business systems and those of their suppliers and trading partners. In particular, they have developed a series of alliances, collaborative ventures and partnerships that generate profit from the professionals who are not directly employed by the company. Such

It is too easy to find yourself concentrating on sourcing products and services. Refocus part of your effort on to defining, locating, accessing and securing the rights to knowledge and intellectual property.

Case Study:
Skandia Insurance
Assessing intellectual capital and its role in business renewal

Since 1994, Sweden's Skandia Insurance Co., whose stock trades in Stockholm, London and Copenhagen, has been publishing supplemental annual reports that attempt to measure intellectual capital by documenting hidden assets such as employee competence, computer systems, work processes, trade marks and customer lists. Its commercial life insurance division, for example, reports not only gross premium income, operating expense ratios and insurance profits, but also a 'satisfied customer index', customer loyalty (measured by the average number of years its policy holders have been customers), market share, total number of employees, the average age of its employees, an employee 'empowerment index',

premium income per salesperson, net claims ratios and training expenses per employee.

Skandia has adopted this approach to help it identify the factors that drive the growth of its business and to make better use of them.

It claims successes – cutting the time it takes to establish a variable annuity business in a new country from about seven years to seven months, for example, and launching a new bank in nine months by combining telemarketing techniques from its car insurance business with a customer database from its life insurance business. All of this demonstrates the power of understanding and leveraging critical intellectual assets both in-house and across the services supply chain.

relational strategies are explicitly included within their measurement framework.

Without doubt there is a need for more thorough frameworks of measurement and definition of intellectual capital. Brooking's classification of four widely accepted categories can be readily applied to supply chain strategy:

- **market assets**, i.e. brands, customers, franchises, licensing agreements, and the products of collaborative supplier relationships;
- **infrastructure assets**, i.e. systems, processes, management philosophies and corporate culture, both internally within a company and with inter-dependent third parties;
- **human centred assets**, i.e. the value of a flexible and market responsive workforce, together with the competencies of external suppliers and trading partners;
- **intellectual property assets**, i.e. patents, trade marks, copyrights, trade secrets and the contractual and legal processes used to protect them.

Many researchers in this area have estimated that less than 25% of such assets are being utilized effectively. Clearly, if this situation is correct, companies are not achieving their full performance and profitability because they do not know how to define, channel and exploit them, both within their own business and across the supply chain. The emerging field of knowledge management is about the different ways in which companies can address this weakness in capability by placing a greater emphasis on the creation, sharing, storage and exploitation of their employees' knowledge, as well as the expertise of their trading partners. It is about harnessing such knowledge for value creation and profit purposes. Clearly this needs new approaches and structures. The following areas are likely to prove of substantial benefit across the supply chain:

- invest in technology and the electronic supply chain to facilitate rapid transfer of knowledge across the business via internal web sites, intranets and group ware;
- invest equally in inter- and intra-team processes within the company and with trading partners. This should

include a substantial expansion in joint programmes of
training and development;

■ make staff and suppliers responsible for the development and sharing of knowledge: target and incentivize
this area;

■ maintain a strong focus on new product development.
Managing knowledge is one part of the equation;
creating it is the other. 3M is a role model through the
15% rule which allows staff to spend that amount of
time on development projects and the governing principle that 25% of company turnover must come from
products introduced in the last four years;

■ develop an audit process for the commercial evaluation
of the value of knowledge;

■ establish the market value of your intellectual property;

■ build that evaluation into the operating processes and
relational strategies applied within collaborative
relationships with major suppliers.

A case study in preferential positioning: fear, greed and desire

Markets for natural commodities are often regarded as being
beyond the reach of proactive supply chain strategy. They
are seen as not being responsive to rational supply market
interventions. It is as though elemental commercial forces
are at work which cannot be controlled or constrained.
Price and value are deemed to be controlled by 'the market'.
This fundamentally misunderstands how such markets
operate; particularly when major swings in sentiment occur
within and across their supply chains.

We will use the challenge of volatile commodity
markets to demonstrate that strategic supply chain thinking
can have a dramatic impact on both price and value propositions. Leveraging any change in this area is a real test of
high level procurement and relational competence, but it
most certainly can be achieved.

The 'market victim' excuse for inactivity

Commodity markets, by definition, are driven by the competing forces of supply and demand. If supply outstrips demand then prices are depressed. This may typically be due to the addition of new capacity or a downturn in demand triggered by negative perceptions of future economic activity. Similarly, if demand outstrips supply then prices are forced up. This may be due to the accelerating pace of economic activity or disruption in supply through production failure, changes in stockholding, short-term fluctuations in capacity due to plant maintenance needs, accidents and natural calamities.

Unless your organization requires very substantial volumes of a given commodity, it is not possible to control directly the macro cyclical movements in commodity prices that occur due to the supply and demand drivers described above. But that is not a justification for the 'market victim' reaction which is frequently used to justify inactivity. Concerted action by multiple small to medium sized purchasers of a commodity can have a significant bearing on the micro detail of a commodity price cycle. Equally, individual action, on a highly confidential basis, can create a competitive advantage in the market place.

Understand the value drivers: fear, greed and desire

The typical dynamics of a commodity market are shown in Figure 2.3. They reveal the cyclical influences on price for any given traded commodity. Start at low pricing and move clockwise around the circle.

When prices are at the low point in the cycle, 'noise' begins to be heard in the market. This is usually triggered by producers in an attempt to stimulate price acceleration. This noise typically has little basis in fact. It hints at supply shortage. Rumours such as potential restrictions in available supply capacity or the severity of man-made or natural disasters fuel the commodity drivers. Examples are plentiful: maybe a strike at a large mine, or an explosion at a major propylene plant, or the need to decommission several aluminium smelters for essential maintenance. There may be active collaboration by producers in a collusive manner. Suppliers begin to eliminate capacity or put investment on hold.

The manifestation of these drivers is panic buying to overcome fears of shortages. This involves purchasers placing forward orders to increase their stock holding. The noise and rumours have triggered this reaction. There is

Figure 2.3

Too many organizations are just carried along by the rollercoaster ride of commodity markets. The need is for proactivity

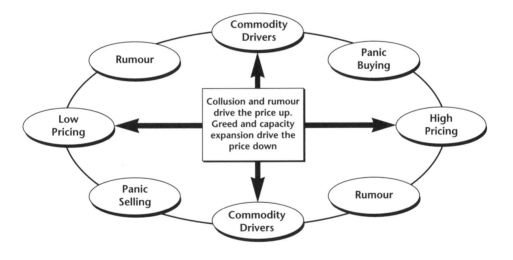

now an anticipation that prices will move higher due to the perception, created by the rumours, of imminent changes in the supply–demand balance. The act of increasing demand through forward ordering then, of course, creates the situation that buyers were trying to avoid. Suppliers now use the pricing and shortage situation to boost sales and ramp up their profits.

The converse is true when prices are high. A different type of 'noise' can be detected in the market place. Suppliers attempt to prolong the shortage rumours to

Commodity markets are a stark example of the powerful forces of fear, greed and desire that drive many supply chain commercial transactions. Rather than being driven along in a reactive fashion, the need is to develop a more appropriate approach to the market. The goal is then to secure a preferential position on both price and value.

maintain artificially high pricing. Insiders and dealers attempt to manipulate and control the supply. The effect is to stimulate the commodity drivers. Different factors of influence then apply. These may induce new entrants into the market, hoping to capitalize on the high prices. Return on investment decisions are now based on attractive pricing. Capacity is increased to take advantage of the favourable pricing regime. Such factors cause suppliers to over-produce. Supply soon exceeds demand. Rumours start. Maybe there has been an exciting discovery of a new, easily recoverable ore body; or a concern that stock forecasts of traded metal have been overstated; or a major new source of material, probably in the former Soviet Republics or China, is soon to be unleashed on to the free world market.

All this 'noise' generates an expectation that the supply–demand balance will tilt in favour of the buyer and cause prices to fall. This triggers in suppliers the desire to sell quickly and capture the currently available high prices. Equally, buyers will often withhold orders in the expectation of lower prices in the future. Sellers panic. Prices fall in a forlorn attempt to stimulate sales.

Research into any commodity market demonstrates that they follow historical patterns with 'exceptional events' triggering considerable variations. Commodity supply is not necessarily cost based. Suppliers are prepared to sustain several years of marginal activity to reap the benefits of the boom year. This creates the 'buyer is a victim of the market' paradigm which most organizations accept. Suppliers do not acknowledge any accountability for pricing either, and claim that they are also controlled by the market. And yet, as can be seen in Figure 2.4, there are a number of proactive market management interventions available. So, what can be done to break the traditional cycle?

The traditional approach to commodity management is to 'beat the market'. It is based on best guess and market intelligence of supply and demand forces. It is not based on cost or value. Commodities are traded on buyer perception, rumour from producers and close relationships with sellers. Buyers derive satisfaction and some success by knowing the market. They try to minimize their degree of market victimization but they are still trapped within the dominant paradigm. A second approach, hedging, also accepts the premise of the market rate and operates within these parameters. It is only a means of protection against financial loss by a counterbalancing transaction. It does nothing to influence the market. Equally, using options is a similar method of operation that remains within the market paradigm. They secure the right to purchase a commodity at a fixed price at a later date.

Figure 2.4

Breaking the traditional cycle of influence involves stepping outside the commodity paradigm and managing the market

US Commodities	Key Facts on the Commodities	Typical Interventions
Cheese	• Trading on Green Bay commodity exchange • A few traders in control • Unsubstantiated premiums	• Develop cost based not market based pricing • Challenge all premiums • Develop a key strategic alliance
Meat	• Trades through a broker network • Few key players. Vertically integrated control in the supply chain • High volatility	• Minimize the middle men • Develop a strategic relationship with the supply chain controllers • Develop alternative pricing

Supply conditioning is a more proactive, if tactical, attempt to counter the fear, greed and desires of the market. It is a determination to guard against being conditioned by suppliers when prices are low and an equal determination to do the same to the supply base when prices are high. With strong nerves it can have considerable success (and failure). The 1997 turmoil in South East Asian financial markets presented many such opportunities across a wide range of industrial commodities. An extension of conditioning is single sourcing. This is when the buyer takes a conscious decision to source from only one supplier, irrespective of the market price. In the short term, a price

When buyers try to beat the market they fail to realize that they have actually accepted the dominant paradigm. At best they achieve only temporary comparative advantage over competitors. What is needed is a determination to make more direct interventions capable of delivering a preferential and sustainable position.

premium may have to be paid, in excess of the best spot price available. The immediate goal is to signal that a different approach to pricing is being adopted. It may condition the market that the general level of pricing is about to turn downwards. Principles on future pricing are then agreed with the supplier.

However, the most powerful approach is to step outside the dominant market paradigm. The goal is then to act on the commodity price rather than react to the market price. It is an extension and more creative option of single sourcing. The requirement is to align with specifically targeted, non-colluding producers to determine a pricing method which is not in line with the market mentality. There is absolutely no intention of disturbing or changing the entire commodity market. By achieving a unique position, competitive advantage can be secured. Secrecy and confidentiality are, not surprisingly, of paramount importance. Three typical interventions are used:

- **Formula pricing**. This is based on the premise that all commodities can be costed by material, labour, overhead and profit. It also assumes that a supplier may find it advantageous to secure a fixed volume of business at a predictable level of profit rather than be 'victimized' by the market. The goal is then to locate a supplier who will forgo some boom profits for guaranteed coverage of fixed costs on a year by year basis.

- **Rebate pricing**. The need is to locate a supplier who is willing to work with you, on a confidential basis, into the longer term. The guiding principle of the relationship is competitive advantage for your company while the market price is applied to other customers. In return for long-term business, the supplier provides an ongoing and exclusive rebate to you.

- **Historical pricing with caps**. There are two versions. Firstly, when average price is capped on the upside and downside so that both parties assume and share some of the risk. Secondly, it can be agreed that pricing will move in increments from a position that is different to the market base. So, for example, if the market increases by 2%, your price increases by only 1%. If the market goes down by 2%, your price reduces by 1%. Behind this agreement, both parties then strive to find operational efficiencies that can deliver a cost advantage.

Direct interventions within supply markets can dramatically transform the bottom line. Realizing the benefits, though, requires high levels of senior executive support, determination to develop sourcing strategies, and a readiness to manage the consequent risk.

The profitability of many manufacturing businesses is closely dependent on the pricing of the commodities that are incorporated into their products and brands. Inertial market behaviour can directly and dramatically erode margins and earnings per share. Some organizations, like Curtice Burns Foods, have been prepared to pursue a strategy of more active market management. While the final illustrations in this chapter have been from natural commodities, that message applies to many sectors.

Case Study:

Curtice Burns Foods

Transforming volatile commodity purchasing by active market management

Stephen Wright, Curtice Burns Executive Vice President, believes that 'Strategic supply chain management is the one key to success in managing volatile agricultural commodities.' Recent initiatives in his business confirm the accuracy of this statement.

Curtice Burns operates in a supply chain where supply–demand economics, shortages, weather, government regulation and cartels are the essence of the management challenge. Success with such volatile agricultural commodities depends on developing strong analytical approaches to supply chain management. Working with major meat suppliers, Curtice Burns was able to redesign its processing area, develop new specifications and create formulas which allow suppliers

and Curtice Burns to achieve competitive advantage, consistent supplies, and price stability in an inherently volatile market.

Working with its edible oil suppliers, Curtice Burns developed a cost based formula to minimize volatility, provide least cost pricing and ensure adequate profit for the suppliers. This change allowed commodity stability to be achieved, and secured competitive advantage for Curtice Burns.

The company now manages its supply business by creating two to three year source plans for all of its major categories of expenditure. Such effective long-range planning has enabled Curtice Burns to achieve over $26 million in cost reduction in three years.

Leveraging value across the supply chain – action checklist

Activities to launch straight away

1. Review current value propositions to customers and evaluate the appropriateness of price vs. functionality.
2. Assess the strength of the external focus on to customer needs as the prime driver of value delivery.
3. Determine the significant gaps in new product development and define a planned programme of innovation.
4. Reconsider the appropriate involvement of third parties and suppliers within this product development cycle.
5. Sponsor a high level team to assess the value of intellectual capital and strategic capabilities.
6. Invest in technology and the electronic supply chain to allow rapid transfer of knowledge across the business.
7. Scrutinize the market management strategies of the company in areas impacted by volatile commodities.

Initiatives to make a significant difference

1. Launch top level teams to define the future markets for products or services, and the strategies to achieve a pre-eminent or dominant position within them.
2. Define these strategies in terms of differentiation, innovation and cost leadership.
3. Assess the strategic capabilities which must be resourced, developed, protected and leveraged ahead of competitors.
4. Exploit the market value of intellectual property.
5. Invest in inter- and intra-team processes within the company and with trading partners in order to target and highlight the incentives of utilizing such exploitation.
6. Determine the processes that will enable the exercise of power and influence over each step in the supply chain.
7. Appropriate value through the exercise of such power.

CHAPTER THREE

Redefining the boundaries of business

Overview

1. Vertical integration vs. deverticalization
2. Restructuring of assets and capabilities
3. Modular, network and virtual sourcing
4. Strategic capability assessment
5. Make–buy and outsourcing
6. Innovation and new product development
7. Suppliers as a source of innovation
8. Role of supplier and purchaser development
9. Access to, and control of, technological capabilities
10. Upstream supply chain management

The Bottom Line

External supplier management is assuming more strategic significance as companies become reliant on third parties. Decisions to increase dependency on external sources, in manufacturing, for product development and through outsourcing, require a robust assessment of capabilities.

Deverticalization and restructuring of assets and capabilities

Many sectors and businesses are in strategic turmoil. The 1990s have witnessed a partial deconstruction of past organizational and structural arrangements as leading companies have vigorously pursued acquisitions, divestment, strategic alliances, joint ventures, partnerships, outsourcing and business swaps as they shift from vertically integrated mass production to less rigid, more flexible and responsive forms of operation. Without doubt, substantial corporate restructuring is taking place on an unprecedented scale.

Four linked themes can be detected. Firstly, organizational restructuring, downsizing, delayering and consequent realignment of business units and internal processes was a notable feature of the recessionary years as companies attempted to shift a greater percentage of their fixed cost base into more variable cost structures. Inevitably, this approach resulted in considerable job reductions. Secondly, portfolio restructuring has accelerated with some fundamental changes occurring in the asset base of many companies. Divestment, brand sales, business swaps, spin-offs and buy-backs characterize this approach. Thirdly, a clear view has emerged that successful organizations of the future should be prepared to rely more significantly on their external sources of supply. This, in turn, is challenging the definitions of which capabilities, activities, functions and processes are central to a business, where the boundaries should be drawn, and what a company should or should not own and control. Fourthly, and clearly underpinning many of the other themes, is the prevailing and dominant theory that the real purpose of strategy is the pursuit of focus and the development and protection of those differentiating features which can deliver and sustain both competitive and customer advantage. The essence of this strategic perspective is that companies should only do what they are good at, concentrate on their strategic capabilities, and unbundle, demerge, delayer, divest and outsource everything else. This perspective is represented in graphical form in Figure 3.1. It raises fundamental questions and concerns on the framing of strategic intent.

- What is the core business, how is it defined and how may it change in the future?
- What secures and delivers competitive edge?
- What are the real strategic capabilities of the business: the skills, knowledge sets, resources and assets which enable the co-ordination and integration of complex technologies and processes across a wide diversity of business activities and markets?

'You have to be mad to build more factories when factories already exist.' William R. Johnson, CEO, H.J. Heinz, on the need to reassess capital productivity in the context of business growth.

Figure 3.1

Boundaries of business are defined in the context of what provides a continuing competitor and customer advantage

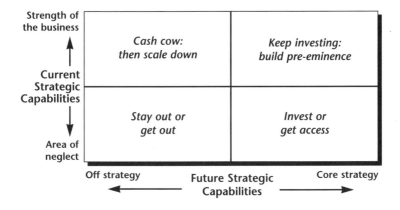

- How can they be developed, strengthened and protected as the prime source of business advantage?
- What is the role of third parties in complementing these strategic capabilities?
- What is the most efficient and productive use of capital to sustain them?

The importance of these questions is not always properly understood. Too many decisions, often with a critical bearing on the shape, focus and direction of a company, are taken in a haphazard fashion, using short-term criteria

Figure 3.2

A number of models of effective integration with suppliers have to be considered, as do the criteria guiding their application

Model 1: Vertical Integration and Traditional Sourcing

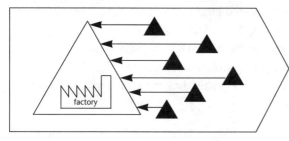

Features	• Vast majority of manufacture done in house. • Arm's length relationship to the supply base.
Criteria	• Use where supply capabilities poor or non-existent. • Relevant for highly confidential and/or proprietary production.

Model 2: Vertical Integration and Modular Sourcing

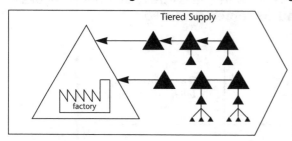

Features	• Assembly still in house but greater use of bought in components. • Complete modules purchased from first tier suppliers.
Criteria	• Secure access to supply from superior supplier capabilities. • Where components and suppliers can be readily segmented.

Model 3: Vertical Disintegration and Network Sourcing

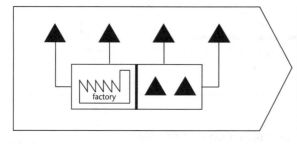

Features	• Apply a mix of in-house and out of house production. • Complete delegation of substantial manufacture to network suppliers.
Criteria	• Systematic evaluation of strategic vs. secondary capabilities. • Sufficient confidence in non-exploitative network relationships.

Model 4: Vertical Disintegration and Virtual Sourcing

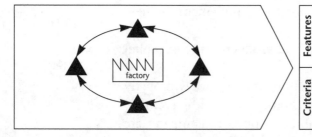

Features	• Minimal or zero manufacture done by the original producer. • Total reliance on linked third parties.
Criteria	• Product development and design capabilities can be controlled. • Required for rapid market penetration and scale up.

(usually framed from a narrow financial perspective) and in an opportunistic manner. Decisions on the boundaries of business, and determining which alternative organizational options to pursue, will have significant impact on both near term profitability and long-term competitive strength. They need to be part of a coherent resourcing strategy and require, in terms of managing third parties, relational competence of a high order. This is a theme which will be pursued in much more detail in Chapter Four.

Deverticalization is about trading fixed costs for more variable costs. It is a switch from inertia to responsiveness. Then start focusing more on what your customers want than merely on productivity benchmarks with competitors. Finally, attack the variable cost base via innovative sourcing strategies.

From vertical integration to virtual sourcing

Many companies have devoted much effort in the past decade to becoming operationally efficient. They are now increasingly turning their attention to more effective use of their capital. Even in industries which have traditionally retained full control over their assets and capabilities there is evidence of an unbundling of businesses and a much greater readiness to utilize the expertise and technologies of suppliers and other third parties. This is hardly surprising since in the maturing economies there can now be found a denser and increasingly capable network of local, regional and global suppliers with high levels of technological sophistication and advanced ways of working. As Figure 3.2 illustrates, we are seeing a gradual disintegration of many traditional vertical and rigid structures in favour of greater interdependence of operation. However, it should not be assumed that all businesses will become virtual. As we will see throughout this chapter, there are guiding criteria that determine how far disintegration should be taken.

Vertical integration occurs when a single enterprise draws all of the activities performed by independent operators into its sphere of operation. The majority of links in the external supply chain are removed. Strong corporate, central control and tight internal co-ordination of functional activities are emphasized. Relationships with third parties, if they exist at all, are at arm's length. This model is traditionally found within new industries and provides:

'This is not a typical restructuring. It's not about plant closures and redundancies. This is a plan to 'deverticalize' the company.' John Bryan, CEO, Sara Lee.

- scale economies and combined operations;
- control over uncertainties of production and supply;
- protection of proprietary knowledge;
- creation of competitive entry barriers;
- bargaining power with suppliers.

The approach works well at a time of rising volumes and premium prices. But it needs the benefits of scale to overcome the operating downsides of inflexibility, inertia and high capital requirements. Once volumes turn downwards, or customers require more responsive and tailored products, then the risk of operating at inefficient levels of production imposes a need for a measure of deverticalization, as can be seen in the Sara Lee case study.

Modular and network sourcing are a clear indication of the departure from vertical integration. There is an acceptance of the need, balanced with an understanding of

---

Case Study:
Sara Lee
Deverticalization and outsourcing of consumer product manufacture

Sara Lee is a global food and consumer products company producing goods such as Kiwi polish, Coach leather products and L'eggs hosiery. They decided in 1997 to dispense with over $3 billion worth of assets across their smaller business units as part of a drive to focus on the business activities that they do best. They believe that their prime strategic capabilities are in brand management, retail relationships and, to a lesser extent, distribution. The result is that they no longer need to own all of their manufacturing assets in order to deliver their brand strategies. The revenue streams affected cover, for example, textile and lingerie products.

They are selling off a number of production units to third parties and then contracting with the new owners for the required supply lines. This restructuring will release cash currently tied up in low margin activities and reduce future need for capital expenditure on manufacturing facilities. It will save $500 million in cash flow terms over three years.

A three stage process was adopted: from 1994 to 1997, the focus was to sort out the internal manufacturing and supply lines first; divest during 1997 and 1998; then retain considerable influence over the new owners by remaining as the dominant customer.

the risks, for greater reliance on external supplier contribution. There may be a tiering of supply as different levels of suppliers become involved in specialized inputs into the outsourced assembly of either the modules or complete systems, platforms and products. The aim is to achieve the benefits of integration while avoiding many of the costs through long-term contracts, close supplier relationships and, on occasions, equity investment. However, this is still quasi-integration. In theory, of course, all of the functions performed within a business can be undertaken by independent suppliers. Until recently, few companies were prepared to consider such virtual supply. This is where third parties co-ordinate all of the necessary economic activities that ultimately deliver value to customers outside the traditional boundaries of the business.

Electronic commerce allows companies to disaggregate a number of the functions and capabilities required in production. Reduced transaction costs may prompt even greater outsourcing to external specialists elsewhere in the supply chain. This needs to be balanced with a rigorous analysis of the potential risks, using the framework of strategic capability assessment.

There is some evidence that this is changing. In particular, electronic commerce and its associated enhancements to inter- and intra-organizational communication, which will be examined in Chapter Nine, may now be removing the previous cost advantage of in-house managed co-ordination of production by slashing the transaction costs involved in sourcing such activities. But, as is emphasized in Figure 3.3, such decisions need to be taken in the context

Figure 3.3

Sourcing strategies and make–buy decisions should be based on a thorough assessment of potential future vulnerability

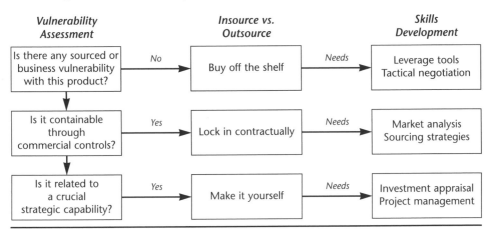

Case Study:
BBC
Radical programming or outsourcing itself out of existence?

The British Broadcasting Corporation (BBC) entered the 1990s as the most influential of the world's media organizations. It had an enviable reputation for creative individuality, supreme production craft skills, moral integrity and strong commitment to an ethos of public service broadcasting.

But at the same time it was faced with a number of stark competitive threats. Technologies, outlets and media channels are changing and expanding rapidly. There is a host of alternative delivery mechanisms through video and computers. New digital transmission techniques and multi-media devices offer the customer a wide array of more exotic new services, while costs of commissioning and producing such mass appeal programmes climb inexorably. Future competition will come not from cosy British companies, but from global giants such as News Corporation, Time Warner, Sony, Matsushita and Microsoft; organizations with access to cash that the BBC could only dream about.

John Birt, the Director General, decided that the BBC could either accept a slow but genteel decline, or fundamentally redefine its way of operating. Despite huge staff resistance, and some ineptly handled change programmes, he chose to pursue the latter option.

1. *'Producer Choice'* was launched. This gave production departments the freedom to buy creative and technical services on the open market. It challenged the notoriously over-staffed bureaucracy of the BBC's resources department. While it was actively resisted, it saved over £0.25 billion for reinvestment in programme making. For the first time, creative staff had to come to terms with commercial and cost transparent approaches.

2. Programme production was separated from commissioning and scheduling. This structural change has become part of a broader intent to create a 'publisher broadcaster' whose purpose is to commission excellent programming from outside production companies. This will take the BBC in the direction of focusing on programmes rather than the hardware that produces them.

Birt's vision is a reconstruction of the BBC. It will focus on the single strategic capability of commissioning. Every other aspect of the broadcasting business can be farmed out. The end game may be the BBC applying the concept of the virtual corporation.

of potential future vulnerability for the business. However, an increasing number of organizations do seem prepared to accept proportionately greater risk in the context of redefining and refocusing their strategies. This is certainly at the heart of John Birt's approach to the BBC.

'It is about not trying to invent everything. Ninety per cent of what you do, someone out there can do better.' John Brophy, General Manager, Corporate Research, BP Chemicals, on outsourcing technology.

Capability assessment to minimize vulnerability

One of the challenging requirements of business is to balance internal capability control with external access to supplier capabilities. The role of suppliers in this area is summarized in Figure 3.4. The degree to which any company should insist on retaining control over its core technologies, assets and capabilities will clearly depend on the nature of the industry, its location, overall maturity of

Figure 3.4

Managing deverticalisation and strategic outsourcing requires supplier development capabilities and high order contractual skills

Strategy Drivers	Preferred Approach	Skills Required	Expected Deliverables
Focus & Simplicity	Divest off-strategy, secondary capabilities. Redirect internal resources on to prime tasks.	Assess market place, supply chain and competitor-led vulnerabilities. Link rewards and incentives to core strategy accomplishment.	Operational delivery aligned to core business strategies. Congruence of mission, leadership, performance and compensation.
Capital Productivity	Channel capital into identified strategic capabilities. Enforce capital investment decisions that focus on to the core business.	Top down–bottom up definition of current and emergent capabilities. Audit of capital investment policy and evaluation of investment pay-off.	Investment appraisal process supportive of future business strategy. Higher return on capital employed in defined strategic segments.
Innovation Flow	Utilize capabilities and expertise of third party providers. Secure innovation from these providers ahead of competitors.	Strategic supplier appraisal using a capabilities approach. Implementation of exclusivity deals and guarantees on non-supply to competitors.	Increase in understanding on required capabilities from third party suppliers. Increase in implemented innovation, ahead of competitors.
Cost Management	Lower fixed cost base and shift to variable costs. Cost transparency and a commitment to year-on-year cost improvement.	Cost benefit analysis of added value contribution. Extension of best practice cost models to suppliers.	Improvement in the ratio of fixed to variable costs. Continuous pipeline of cost improvement ideas.

'The key to making such deals work is that each contractor has separate and distinct responsibilities, and that the companies concerned are ethical, that they communicate, and that they have the client's best interests at heart.'
George Shaheen, CEO, Andersen Consulting, on collaborating with competitors.

the sector and its supply network. Since companies are defined by the activities in which they excel, the goal should always be to understand these fully, through systematic strategic assessment, followed by a concentration of capital and resources on to those strategic capabilities where a pre-eminent position can be built and protected. Make–buy analysis and outsourcing can then be made within the context of such strategic decision criteria. Examples are provided from Du Pont and Shell to demonstrate the need for such an assessment. The proper and realistic evaluation of the following issues needs to occur:

- recognize that co-ordination by the market rather than through internal hierarchy has potentially serious risks and disadvantages as well as benefits;

Case Study:

Du Pont
Accessing technological skills while splitting roles and accountabilities for IT

Du Pont, the global chemicals and energy company, outsourced its information technology operations to Computer Sciences Corporation and Andersen Consulting in one of the biggest deals of its kind. It is worth $4 billion over ten years.

Under the arrangement, 2,600 staff of Delaware based Du Pont were transferred to CSC with another 500 going to Andersen. About 1,100 information systems employees, including the management team responsible for developing and maintaining corporate IT standards, however, remain in-house.

The move was designed to improve cost effectiveness, enhance business processes, streamline systems and increase productivity. But, equally importantly, the whole arrangement has been designed to avoid one of the key problems emerging with outsourcing. Du Pont has retained the position of being the lead integrator.

This will ensure appropriate focus. At times, commercial pressure will also need to be applied on to their outsourcing suppliers to ensure that they apply their best people and total expertise to Du Pont's needs. According to Linda A. Hallman, Chief Information Officer at Du Pont, it will also enable them 'to work together with the best of the best'; a clear goal being the strengthening of their technology capability through external access.

- retain an unwavering in-house vertical integration policy over products, services and capabilities where you are confident that you possess and can sustain a long-term proprietary advantage;
- if that cannot be attained, for financial or business expansion reasons, then ensure that very tight control is exercised with closely managed suppliers;
- be exceptionally wary of the loss of control over critical strategic capabilities and be sceptical of the ability of contractual arrangements or intellectual property law to provide adequate safeguards;
- outsourcing and the integration of third party suppliers always poses strategic, managerial and operational challenges – expect the worst, and plan for it;
- avoid outsourcing becoming a means of dealing with troublesome peripheral activities – sort the function out before you subcontract it;
- retain in-house expertise to manage the overall process.

You cannot outsource outsourcing. Strategic issues and operational problems need to be properly addressed by executive management. Don't expect any improvement simply by handing a problem over to a third party. Since the market is still immature, it is vital to retain a measure of control and protection over the future. Build that into your contracts with suppliers.

Case Study:
Shell

Transferring control of non-petrol logistics to a third party

Shell UK decided that it needed to take drastic action with its non-petrol forecourt suppliers.

Its petrol stations sell a wide array of branded products, foodstuffs, drinks and similar grocery or household items. While this market has expanded rapidly, many of the logistical routines and delivery procedures had also driven up the levels of disruption and complexity. A typical site would receive up to 40 deliveries a week from 15 different distributors. Not surprisingly, this is very difficult to co-ordinate and soaks up a lot of site management time in scheduling, controlling and checking.

The Shell solution was to rationalize distribution. A specialist logistics company was awarded a £100 million, five year contract covering 90% of the business to handle distribution of non-petrol goods to its 850 sites. The contract ensured that deliveries to each site would drop to around seven. Staff time is reduced by about eight hours a week. Savings amount to 2-3% of the gross profits of individual sites.

Shell decided, though, to retain control over delivery of fuel. Safety and service were deemed to be an internal core competence and were not outsourced.

Innovation and new product development

Globalization of markets, shorter product life cycles, deregulation, emerging sources of competition within South America and Asia Pacific, the relentless pace of business change, new models of co-operation in the form of interdependence between erstwhile competitors and, in particular, more discerning and discriminating customers are encouraging (or more likely, forcing) many companies to refocus on the opportunities for business growth that innovation can deliver.   Increasingly, and particularly after the downsizing and delayering of the recessionary years, there is a growing recognition that strategies of operational improvement and organizational effectiveness alone are not a substitute for the enhanced earnings that can be delivered from revenue growth. This needs to be fuelled by either adapting and broadening current products and services through range extensions, or by committing to new and highly differentiated offerings to the customer. This is an important distinction. Three principal types of innovation can be detected:

- type one: blue sky pioneer products;
- type two: 'me too' imitative products;
- type three: adaptive product extensions.

Incremental, adaptive innovation is a strategy characterized by 'the more new products, the better'. It is a relatively low risk approach, calling for modest capital investment.   It does not require fundamental research but the on-going, continuous development of outstanding products that enhance the value proposition to customers and successfully ward off new competitors. As we saw in Chapter Two, the relationship between price and functionality will be crucial. Focusing on such modest innovations, rather than radically new concepts and designs, has sometimes been neglected. In many organizations the research and development paradigm associated with pioneer products and technological leadership has tended to dominate. Yet this can be a most expensive and high risk route. Few companies actually possess the depth of specialized capabilities, technological resources or capital to sustain it. Being a 'fast adapter' may be a much more cost efficient and profitable route to follow. We have termed this a type three innovation strategy, as can be seen in Figure 3.5. Because risk is so low, there should be few objections to involving external suppliers actively in the product development process in conjunction with internal research and development resources.

Type two, 'me too' imitative product development is successful if a company possesses, or can access from third parties, the capability of applying new technology rapidly once it has been tested by a more pioneering innovator. The strategy then becomes one of letting others make the capital investments, encounter the initial teething problems and suffer the costly but inevitable mistakes. It assumes, of course, that it is possible for the imitator to design around

'A good innovator is someone who recognizes market potential, who recognizes a need in the market place, and can put together the technology, the manufacturing, the marketing, the selling and the service to meet that market need.' Ian Harvey, CEO, British Technology Group.

Figure 3.5

Early involvement of suppliers in product development is crucial. But it needs to be carefully related to the nature of the product

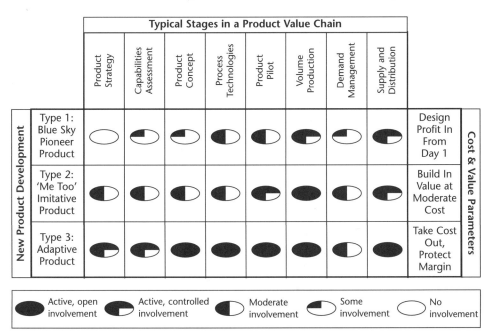

		Typical Stages in a Product Value Chain							
New Product Development		Product Strategy	Capabilities Assessment	Product Concept	Process Technologies	Product Pilot	Volume Production	Demand Management	Supply and Distribution	Cost & Value Parameters
	Type 1: Blue Sky Pioneer Product	No involvement	Some involvement	Some involvement	Moderate involvement	Moderate involvement	Active, controlled	Moderate involvement	Active, controlled	Design Profit In From Day 1
	Type 2: 'Me Too' Imitative Product	Moderate involvement	Moderate involvement	Moderate involvement	Moderate involvement	Active, controlled	Active, open	Moderate involvement	Active, controlled	Build In Value at Moderate Cost
	Type 3: Adaptive Product	Active, controlled	Active, controlled	Active, open	Active, open	Active, open	Active, open	Moderate involvement	Active, open	Take Cost Out, Protect Margin

● Active, open involvement	◗ Active, controlled involvement	◐ Moderate involvement	◝ Some involvement	○ No involvement

the copyright, patents or intellectual property of the original innovator. This is usually straightforward enough in the services sector but can be problematic with some technologically complex products. Again, it is a relatively low to medium risk strategy. The crucial features are the ability and determination to defeat the pioneer through agility, responsiveness, cost and price effectiveness and, particularly, branding.

True innovation involves challenging all your strategic assumptions. Make sure it covers how you think about your industry, your products, your customers and the future. Redefine the boundaries of business. Push back your definitions of customers. Then redraw the map.

The third available strategy of product or service development involves true innovation and is the preserve of the 'blue sky' pioneer product. This usually requires a world beating quantum leap forward. It will be brought about by a fundamental challenge to the prevailing assumptions of business and, as such, often will not occur within conventional R&D teams or processes. Exploiting existing knowledge and technologies fits in well with the penetration of current or adjacent markets. It lends itself to conventional team working since most of the product problems and delivery processes will already have been addressed. It usually does not work well with true innovation. A more chaotic, even subversive, and less structured or hierarchical culture is needed.

A crucial question in the development of any new product or service development strategy is whether the company should be investing the majority of its allocated resources into the technology associated with innovation, or the product's eventual branding; or to split it equally between these two features. The indications from many sectors are that being the technology pioneer does not necessarily confer a sustainable competitive advantage. While it may provide protection against those competitors who do not offer leading edge or innovative products, branding appears to provide competitive protection while also enabling the company to secure premium pricing ahead of that justified on functionality alone.

Equally, and as will be argued in Chapter Six on 'The Responsive Supply Chain', a crucial feature of branding is the ability to deliver the product or service in a way that meets, or even exceeds, the expectations of the end customer. The supply chain must be sufficiently focused on to this goal and fully capable of addressing these needs in a timely, reliable, consistent and responsive fashion while still ensuring that the target profit margin can be sustained. The conclusion, therefore, is that three linked strategies deliver successful new products and services: focused investment in appropriate technology capable of providing a sufficient measure of differentiation through functionality and/or pricing; well planned and thoroughly executed marketing to develop and reinforce the brand proposition with eventual customers; and a supply chain that is aligned and operationally excellent in timely product or service delivery at relatively low cost. The Senco Fasteners case study provides an excellent illustration of this approach. It is also noticeable that this focus on innovation has been secured within such a small company.

As long as your business is investing sufficiently in the technology of innovation, concentrate more of your resources on internal integration of relevant functions across your business, access to external suppliers and the market positioning of the product or service through exemplary branding. Spend the cash on the brand, rather than the R&D laboratories.

Case Study:
Senco Fasteners
Innovation and service delivery across the supply chain

Senco is a privately owned company based in Cincinnati, making industrial staple guns. While this is hardly the most prosaic product, their business approach is outstanding.

They have enshrined a commitment to creativity and innovation within the 'Senco Management Concepts'. This acknowledges that as an organization there are two states of operating: firstly to assure their own survival and secondly to assure their advancement. Most importantly, they recognize that these require different types of function.

The survival side focuses especially on disseminating fundamental business concepts to all staff and suppliers so that they can enhance their contribution and take charge of their own work redesign.

On the advancement side they use Business Development Information Resource Teams to focus on the external supply chain and their product markets. This requires them to produce challenging, creative scenarios and gather the experiential knowledge needed to evaluate them.

Few companies are as committed to harnessing creativity and involving stakeholders as Senco.

Deficiencies of the linear model of innovation

Although the steps in the value chain of innovation and product development, graphically described in Figure 3.5, have been represented in a linear fashion, it is important to emphasize that companies are recommended, in practice, to start at the customer end of the chain and work backwards. Challenge the traditional model whereby the majority of resources and top management attention are concentrated on an internal, inventive, technology led research and development function. The approach whereby R&D develops the technology, which then migrates towards a market need and then finally supports the actual creation of a product to meet that need, is deeply flawed. Rather than initially concentrating on creativity, technology and innovation, it is much more effective to focus on the customers. Start by identifying the likely market and its future needs and then, once real clarity has been achieved, begin to map out the development path. Too many companies address innovation the wrong way around, particularly where they have created research and development centres, often in splendid locations and with superb facilities, that are completely isolated and cocooned away from commercial pressures and demanding customer or operational realities.

*'Mindset is a major issue. All our research people could pass a test on economics; some of them have a very high level of urgency. We just want to change their mindset so that they feel good only if two things happen: they get the job done, and the business they support performs to corporate standards.'
Jim Street, Group Research Coordinator, Royal Dutch Shell.*

Sources of innovation

Traditionally, most organizations have addressed innovation through a mix of the following approaches:

- through in-house research and development resources;
- from reverse engineering, through the systematic breakdown and rebuilding of competitors' products;
- through licensing agreements, usually from overseas competitors and with the right to supply a specific geographical area;
- from design houses and specialist consultancies;
- through strategic alliances and joint ventures;
- through acquisition of a leading edge innovator.

Certainly, the external third party supplier's contribution has been minimal; or it has been linked to a very subordinate support role in response to in-house direction and management. Completion of the assessment chart in Figure 3.6 will soon confirm this situation. However, there is increasing dissatisfaction with this traditionally distant relationship. Increasing competition and the growing complexity of technology in many industries means that it is taking far too long, and at an unsustainable cost, for innovation to be pursued alone. This does not just apply to initial blue sky research. The rule of thumb is that for every $1 spent on such research, $10 will be spent on further development and an additional $100 will be required to exploit the eventual products through manufacture, distribution and marketing on an increasingly regional or global scale. Equally, there have been frequent failures of companies unable to reap the full benefits of their innovative ideas. Internally, there is a need to challenge and break down the cultural and functional divides between different

'I think it's impossible to really innovate unless you can deal with all aspects of a problem. If you can only deal with yolks or whites, it's pretty hard to make an omelette.'
Gene Amdahl, Founder of Amdahl Corporation and Acsys.

Figure 3.6

Capturing and deploying innovation from suppliers ahead of competitors is a neglected area of supply chain transformation

Assess your organization's current performance in innovation capture from suppliers.

1 Not Started	**2** In Its Infancy	**3** Moving Forward	**4** Solid Success	**5** Strength of the Business

Please assess current performance on required processes for innovation capture:

	1	2	3	4	5
1. Business awareness of potential for supplier innovation.	1	2	3	4	5
2. Enthusiasm for suppliers as a source of innovation.	1	2	3	4	5
3. Defined method for innovation capture.	1	2	3	4	5
4. Agreed internal process for responding to innovation.	1	2	3	4	5
5. Joint innovation forums and senior management reviews.	1	2	3	4	5
6. Co-presentations of innovation plans with suppliers.	1	2	3	4	5
7. Agreed objectives and innovation plan of purchase.	1	2	3	4	5
8. On-line feedback to suppliers on innovation delivery.	1	2	3	4	5
9. Audit of internal response to innovative ideas.	1	2	3	4	5
10. Tracking the conversion and deployment of innovation.	1	2	3	4	5

'The answer is not simply to ask scientists to be more innovative. Innovation must be driven by management who know the needs of their business and have the vision to look for new market opportunities and more effective ways of working.' Peter Watson, AEA Technology.

parts of the organization. Too many research and design staff spend a considerable amount of their time on inwardly focused activity rather than looking externally towards the customer. It is worth remembering that suppliers are often much closer to the customer, and they are continually exposed to the ideas and innovations of other companies. Provided the necessary contractual safeguards can be put in place (and the difficulties of this should not be underestimated), they can provide a valuable perspective on future product development, particularly for the imitative and adaptive products. Satisfactory gain sharing and exclusivity arrangements are needed to justify the involvement on the blue sky projects. The Nestlé case study is an example of such an approach. A number of guidelines on joint product development strategies need to be considered, and thoroughly reviewed with potential supplier partners:

Case Study:
Nestlé

Caffeine free coffee: solving a problem – dominating a market

All coffee producing companies face the same problem. How do you reduce the costs of manufacture of decaffeinated coffee? At present, producing caffeine-free coffee requires expensive chemical washing of the processed beans, which also impairs their flavour and smell. Removing caffeine this way costs producers $1 billion a year in the USA alone. The world coffee market is $20 billion a year.

Incremental improvement would take you down the route of tinkering with the technology and trying to raise productivity.

The much more creative route is to grow caffeine-free coffee beans. Which is what Nestlé, the Swiss food company

that makes Nescafé, the world's number-one selling instant coffee, decided to consider. It may enter into a joint venture with ForBio, an Australian biotechnology group specializing in plant genetics. ForBio, with its US partner Integrated Coffee Technologies Inc. (ICTI), have discovered how to alter coffee plant seeds genetically so as to yield caffeine-free beans. Large scale propagation of the plants is under way.

Once the process is proven, Nestlé will strike exclusive purchasing arrangements with coffee producers licensed to grow the genetically altered plants. ForBio and ICTI make their money through licence fees and royalty sales.

- top management to provide a strong vision on the overall direction of innovation and create the conditions to sustain it;
- recognize, however, that breakthroughs rarely come from formal top-down processes. Tolerate a less planned approach on occasions;
- introduce supplier expertise very early in the process. Ideally, the more complex the technology, the earlier the involvement (subject to strict confidentiality);
- ensure that roles are very clearly allocated;
- address the issues of costs and profitability from the beginning of the project;
- consider outsourcing complete processes and technologies provided they are not your strategic capability;
- research and design steps to be done concurrently rather than sequentially as far as possible;
- ensure that innovations are thoroughly protected by intellectual property patenting and licensing agreements for their exploitation.

'Any intelligent corporate strategy must have innovation at its very heart.'
Walter Kunerth, Executive Vice President, Siemens.

A crucial role for supplier and purchaser development

Throughout these initial chapters we have argued that business development strategies, innovation, deverticalization (under certain carefully evaluated conditions), capability access and revenue growth are the touchstones of organizational success. Building new revenue streams calls for a committed focus on a combination of four available strategic options:

- extension of business into adjacent markets;
- organic growth within existing markets;
- growth by acquisition, strategic alliances and joint ventures;
- innovation, either in product and service development or in the creation of more effective distribution or supply channels in order to create an entirely new market.

Invariably this requires considerable support from third parties and strategic suppliers: those who possess the essential capabilities to enable such business development strategies to take place. Few organizations have the skills, resources or capital to pursue the necessary combination of innovation, sales growth and market penetration without drawing on these external capabilities. An example from one area, access to technology, is provided in Figure 3.7 to illustrate the need for assessment and alignment of marketing approaches between those purchasers and suppliers who are striving to gain competitive advantage through the control and leveraging of their technical capabilities.

The subject of definition of appropriate relational strategies to secure such capabilities will be addressed in more detail in Chapter Four.

Targeting suppliers with the necessary capabilities

Success in this area calls for strategic supplier and purchaser development. This is about structuring and supporting a programme of capability based activity that will impact those suppliers who are able to deliver significant additional competitive advantage but who will not necessarily do so without active and intensive management. It also calls for a preparedness by the purchaser to review their strengths and weaknesses. Frequently, the target suppliers will be found in one of four categories:

- suppliers considered to be of strategic importance to the business;
- suppliers under contracts in excess of three years;
- monopoly suppliers, or those who are part of an oligopoly;
- suppliers currently involved in major business development programmes.

It should be emphasized that some suppliers may have to be included even though they are either actively hostile to your business aims or, at best, ambivalent towards them. The remit of strategic supplier development may need to involve them, within the short to medium term, even if the desired outcome is the eventual termination of the commercial relationship. Also, it is important to recognize that many suppliers involved in the programme will often possess greater expertise, technical or process capabilities than the sponsoring purchasing organization. After all, this is the reason why they have been targeted in this way. There is a consequent need for a fundamental realignment of some traditional purchasing practice. Avoid heavy handed, arrogant or overly dominant behaviour. Be prepared to pursue a more open and collaborative approach. Recognize that some negative feedback is likely

Examine the behaviour of your organization through the eyes of the supplier who would be most critical of the way you operate. Why not involve them in this searching appraisal?

Figure 3.7

Competitive advantage can be secured through access to and joint control of technological capabilities with suppliers

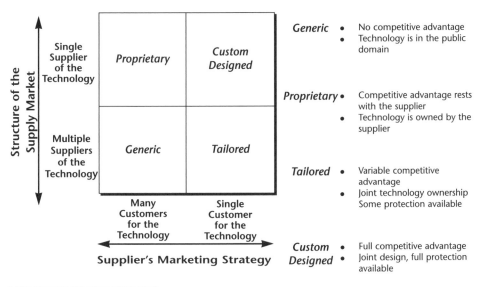

© ADR International Purchasing Consultants

to be received from the supplier. Indeed, be suspicious if that does not happen. The ideal is a constructive but assertive challenge from both sides on their expectations and requirements. Finally, of course, ensure that it is clear which capabilities need to be developed and incorporated within the joint development programme.

Four process issues can then be addressed: allocation of roles and responsibilities; capability gap analysis; shaping of supplier expectations and perceptions; and upstream supply chain management. The McDonalds case study illustrates such a programme of supplier development and its role within an initiative designed to build sales volume and boost profitability.

Allocation of roles and responsibilities

Strategic supplier development begins with real definition and clarity over the potential contribution that is being sought from third parties. The need for explicit linkage between business needs and supplier initiatives has already been emphasized – it is a crucial feature of the approach. Internal organizational facilitation is often required to enable business teams to understand these requirements and the range of options available. Top quality functional professionals have an important role to play in this area as they orchestrate the prime contact points with suppliers. There is usually a need for careful control of information at this stage, since re-sourcing may need to take place. Such staff should be responsible for managing these information flows and channels of communication. There are two requirements:

- **strategic communication:** concentrating on the framing of agendas, exploration of joint synergies, appreciation of business plans and aspirations, and the forging of shared values and common objectives;
- **operational communication:** involving functional staff from both parties and designed to concentrate on the implementational detail of the broad agreements mapped out by the senior executives of both sides.

Understanding the capabilities of the parties

Once there is a measure of common understanding between the parties, a more detailed assessment needs to be made of potential business fit and congruence in both strategic and operational terms. The objective is to establish whether the companies have the resources and organisational maturity to integrate their specialist capabilities in a way that has the potential to yield significant additional value to both sides and, if so, to indicate how this should best be addressed. Furthermore, there needs to be an open recognition of where conflicting or contested goals are likely to present problems, and where capability gaps on

'Three bids and a cloud of dust, isn't our method. We look to the heart of the company.' Dave Nelson, Vice President Purchasing, Honda of America.

Case Study:
McDonalds
Using supplier development to fight off competition and build profitability

Competition, particularly in the USA, is tough. McDonalds has a simple answer to the challenge of Burger King, Wendy's, Pizza Hut, Taco Bell and KFC: to be so aggressive and competitive commercially that it is able to leverage its market dominance. To this end it plans to put everyone worldwide within easy reach of a Big Mac.

Although McDonald's still has more restaurants in the USA than abroad, the overseas business is growing much more rapidly. Indeed, 1995 was a turning point when international operating profits exceeded those of the USA for the first time. The tally is now over 7,500 restaurants in 89 countries outside the domestic US market.

In order to maintain volume and profit growth, McDonalds is placing greater emphasis on the procurement arrangements of its international operations. It is committed increasingly to move from local/regional to regional/global sourcing of raw materials and it is prepared to invest significant resources in supplier development to achieve this. Some typical examples:

1. Worldwide sesame seed requirements for buns are sourced from Mexico.

2. Poland has developed to become one of their largest regional suppliers of meat, potatoes and bread.

3. McDonalds will have made a $500 million investment in Brazil by 2000. It is integrating a number of sole source suppliers, Interbakers, Braslom and Brapelco, at a combined, co-located site called 'Foodtown'.

The effect on the bottom line is considerable. Raw materials normally account for 40% of fast food costs. McDonald's procurement strategies have resulted in materials accounting for approximately 30% of their costs.

*'The best business plan
I've ever seen.' Andy
Grove, CEO of Intel, on
sourcing strategies and
supplier development
initiatives.*

either side may exist. The following will need consideration:

- business mission, core values and operating principles;
- market positioning and product strategies;
- regional and global supply ambitions;
- track record on customer retention;
- innovation performance and investment in product development;
- financial strength and financial stability;
- business planning processes and sophistication of models for strategic action;
- current and projected collaborative relationships, alliances and joint ventures;
- projected capacity utilization and the principles for its development;
- human resource policies, including organizational learning, the environment and employment practice;
- approaches to performance measurement.

Shaping supplier expectations

Many suppliers will need to be convinced of the benefits to themselves of participating in this programme of joint development. This will be particularly true if the prevailing way of working, either in the sector or with regard to specific key players, is essentially opportunistic. Board level directors should be involved with their supplier counterparts in affirming their commitment. In so doing they should:

- fully support and endorse the approach through full investment of their time in developing the necessary personal relationships;
- address concerns created by the functional teams working on detailed capability assessment and operational planning;
- positively challenge thinking and practices in joint development;
- celebrate success, and/or censure inappropriate actions or behaviours.

Such active support fosters a strong perception of executive commitment, builds the necessary momentum and generates confidence in the overall approach.

Upstream supply chain management

Without a clear understanding of the value to be delivered by the programme, confidence that both sides have the capability to deliver it and recognition by the supplier of the benefits accruing to them from their participation, then little support can be expected.   However, once this has been achieved through the processes described above, then the final stag – upstream supply chain management – can move forward quickly. The objective is to focus on each stage in the supply chain and specify in detail how performance and ways of working can be measured and improved. This is particularly the case within sectors where tiering of suppliers is common. In such circumstances, the joint development programme needs to be extended beyond the purchaser and first tier supplier (who will usually be providing a major module or even a complete product) and involve the second and third tier suppliers in the upstream supply chain.

Clearly, as the boundaries of business become less distinct, as confidence builds in the capabilities of key strategic suppliers and as companies become more experienced in the location, assessment and joint development of their trading partners, then there will be much greater demand for staff who possess the relational competence necessary to manage such initiatives. This will be addressed in the next chapter.

Redefining the boundaries of business – action checklist

Activities to launch straight away

1. Conduct an operational review of the performance effectiveness of outsourcing across your business.
2. Develop a tactical and strategic outsourcing policy capable of ensuring effective control over suppliers.
3. Use this policy to determine the functional capabilities to be retained in the business vs. outsourcing targets.
4. Evaluate electronic commerce and emerging technology and their impact on the disaggregation of functions.
5. Extend supplier input into a number of adaptive and imitative product development projects.
6. Redesign supplier assessment and appraisal around the capabilities approach.
7. Target a number of strategic suppliers for involvement in a programme of purchaser–supplier development.

Initiatives to make a significant difference

1. Define those capabilities crucial to future strategic operations, and which provide proprietary advantage.
2. Assess the robustness and comprehensiveness of your strategic frameworks in capability terms.
3. Frame the next wave of organizational and portfolio restructuring, business consolidation, make–buy and strategic outsourcing through the capability approach.
4. Evaluate the connection between strategic capabilities, intellectual advantage and human resource policies designed to attract and retain the best staff.
5. Develop a five year strategic vision on outsourcing, together with a structured blueprint for its attainment.
6. Determine the appropriate input of suppliers into new product development and the potential vulnerabilities.
7. Appoint a board director to sponsor the purchaser-supplier development programme.

CHAPTER FOUR

Developing relational competence

Overview

1. The continuum of relational strategies
2. Developing strategic business relationships
3. Criteria for competition and collaboration
4. The role of free market competition
5. Relaxation of competition
6. Collaborative sourcing
7. Assessing the required capabilities
8. Profiling supplier relationships
9. The development and decline of relationships
10. Capability access through global sourcing

The Bottom Line

Achieving business success through relational effectiveness is an important competence in both organizational and individual terms. It will provide competitive and collaborative advantage. But remember that effective relationships are still the means to an end and not the end itself.

Developing strategic business relationships

Significant changes are occurring worldwide in business-to-business relationships. Many long-established values, beliefs, practices, tools and techniques in corporate management are being challenged and questioned. A wider range of relational types, as can clearly be seen in Figure 4.1, are being considered and applied. The more value adding relationships, often associated with strategic alliances, joint ventures and partnerships, are characterized by the building of fundamentally different ways of working with suppliers and other third parties. They usually involve radical changes in ways of operating for most companies. Achieving business success and competitive advantage through relational effectiveness is becoming an important competence in both organizational and individual terms. Attainment of such competence calls for the application of innovative processes. However, as was emphasized in

Figure 4.1

The appropriate strategy in business to business relationships is defined in the context of access and control over capabilities

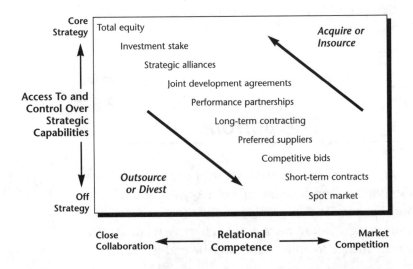

Chapter Three, there has to be a rigorous and balanced evaluation of the reasoning behind the relaxation of market competition and the adoption of more collaborative ways of working.

If any organization is going to derive maximum benefit and real added value from its relationships with third parties, then there has to be a systematic framework for developing, selecting, resourcing and taking them forward through the well defined application of mechanisms for evaluating risks, benefits and required behaviours. The possession of such organizational ability we have termed 'relational competence'. It can reside anywhere in the business, and does not need to be the preserve of any functional group such as purchasing, sales or marketing. But it does need to exist in sufficient depth to ensure the risks of collaboration are contained while maximizing the business development opportunities. This must cover:

- **need**, i.e. the acceptance that a degree of mutual dependence between independent companies in an end market is backed by sound business reasons;
- **fit**, i.e. the integration or close meshing in of complementary and strategic capabilities between several companies to achieve this end market need;
- **values**, i.e. the existence of a necessary level of congruence between the vision, values, ethics and operating styles of potential collaborators;
- **resources**, i.e. the availability of time, capital, staff and infrastructure;
- **management quality**, i.e. the presence of a sufficient level of maturity and competence, in both top management and operational staff required to make the relationships work.

This contrasts with some of the simplistic approaches that were initially adopted as companies experimented with the balance between competitive and collaborative relationships. During this initial development and testing phase there had been a tendency to focus on relationships and commercial behaviour in isolation from the business context in which they were operating.

'True partnership has
been talked about
more than it has
happened so far.' Ian
Canadine, Director-
General, Institute of
Logistics, UK.

A continuum of business relationships

Before examining the crucial question of the criteria that
need to be applied when defining, selecting and reviewing
the effectiveness of business-to-business relationships, it is
important to be fully aware of the principal relational types.
As can be seen in Figure 4.2, there is a continuum in
relationships from the use of free market competition
through to full and active collaboration.

The role of free market competition

Traditionally, the use of free market competition, often
termed competitive leverage in the USA, has been the

Figure 4.2

**Expect to use the full range of relational strategies with third
parties. The key is developing appropriate criteria for their selection**

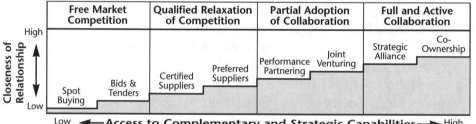

Criteria for Use of Competition		Criteria for Use of Collaboration	
• Over-supply in the market place	• Rapid evolution of innovation	• Complementary capabilities and resources	• Strong and enduring relationships
• Commoditization of products	• Price collapse and cost change	• Access to vital assets and unique innovation	• Shared values and common goals
• Little real market differentiation	• Testing performance capabilities of suppliers	• Required for market access	• Trust earned under fire

Competitive Levers and Strategies		Collaborative Levers and Strategies	
• Volume leverage and regional consolidation	• Market place bench-marking and testing	• Switch to long-term contracting	• Co-investment agreements on marketing
• Aggregate total volumes	• Positional bargaining and negotiation	• Frame transparent performance principles	• Joint funding of research and development
• Use of tactical market manipulation	• Bringing in new sources of supply	• Open book exchange of cost information	• Share sales data and demand forecasts

heartland of tactical purchasing. Such an approach can be readily identified in easy supply markets where there are many competing suppliers to choose from. The purchaser may be spending significant amounts of money. Suppliers may be desperate for the business. Risks are deemed to be low. Little relational sophistication is needed. Simple commercial practices can be applied, usually involving multiple sourcing, frequent and tough negotiation, lots of positioning and bargaining. Full and vigorous use of competition is usually the main lever of persuasion adopted. It is an area characterized by competitive bidding, active use of enquiries, market testing and arm's length tendering. Confrontational and aggressive behaviour is all too frequently encountered. There tends to be little openness and transparency between the parties.

A large number of companies, particularly in the early days of a 'price down' or tactical purchasing improvement programme (this is described in more detail in Chapter Seven), believe that traditional competitive sourcing and assertive management of supplier relationships still have a role to play in certain situations. This tends to be the case when a radical shake-up of a supply market is deemed to be necessary; or where suppliers may have drifted into less competitive positions than could be found in comparison with alternative free market sourcing arrangements; or where so-called partnerships have become cosy, inwardly focused and out-of-touch.

Companies   involved   in   'back-from-the-brink' turnaround situations have been known to use full and vigorous competition as a shock tactic. In such circumstances you are likely to be faced with a need to drive substantial productivity improvements, reduce cost by a major quantum or boost supplier performance dramatically. Invariably, it needs to be done within a very short period of time. This is deemed to justify the employment of very aggressive tactics. Such an approach was adopted by General Motors in the early 1990s through their PICOS teams and the 'programme for improvement and cost optimization of suppliers'. To achieve rapid price breakthroughs, competition and fierce re-bidding of contracts was employed. This was seen as being fully justified in the context of global competition. The goal was to determine which suppliers were prepared to put the customer, General Motors, first in terms of quality, service and, very importantly, price. The mechanism for such an evaluation was fairly unsophisticated bidding.

Extensive use of competition will destabilize a supply chain if the purchaser is a significant player in the market. Having leveraged relationships to the brink, expect a lack of commitment from suppliers in the future, unless you can demonstrate that the exercise was pursued only as a process to locate your future partners.

It achieved considerable turmoil in the supply market. 'Planned' destabilisation took place. Prices from some suppliers went into free fall. Other companies refused to participate. Turbulence was transmitted up and down the automotive components supply chain. Having created a climate of change, as well as fear and resentment, the next phase of the exercise was an attempt to reconsolidate the purchasing operation, strengthen supplier relationships and apply a process of closer integration with the more 'committed' suppliers. These were the ones prepared to embrace the requirements of General Motors and their demanding, or some would argue domineering, approach.

Planned, systematic, competitive leverage still has an important part to play in a number of sourcing situations. It should not be ignored. Market place conditions and business circumstances may require it. Furthermore, this is sometimes the case when it is a carefully controlled element within a programme of purchasing improvement across all of a company's total expenditure. It becomes one approach in the sourcing and relational toolkit. But users do need to be aware of the potential for seriously long lasting damage to supplier relationships. The excessive application of competition rarely induces a desire for open collaboration, product or process development, nor the free exchange of information between supplier and purchaser.

Qualified relaxation of competition

Even in the competitive leverage area it may make sense to concentrate on a smaller number of preferred suppliers, particularly where a business has systematically tested the performance of targeted suppliers through structured appraisal, evaluation and regular benchmarking on prices and performance. This will usually lead to a number of suppliers being approved and certified as meeting the required supply standards.

This type of targeted assessment of supplier capabilities can readily lead to a tiering of potential and actual suppliers against defined criteria. The Nike case example is a typical illustration (but note that the criteria applied turned out to be partial and contained considerable risk to Nike's reputation. This subject is addressed again in Chapter Ten.)

As a result of such an appraisal process, the decision may be taken to relax competition and select a smaller

Framing the criteria for supplier selection and appraisal is often given insufficient thought. A narrow focus is adopted. Criteria may not have been validated. Ensure that you balance sourcing factors with risk, vulnerability and adverse reactions from customers.

Case Study:

Nike

Tiering the supply chain and applying a range of relational strategies

Nike's global success has been supported by a well defined strategy of supplier segmentation.

At the top level of supply, connected to Nike's strategies of product innovation, are their 'developed partners'. These suppliers manufacture the statement products on which future growth and market leadership depends. Initially, this requires low volume production. It is seen as an area for co-development and co-investment in required technologies.

"Volume producers" are selected for their capabilities to deliver high value:low cost products. They are often vertically integrated suppliers but are allowed to produce for other companies under controlled circumstances.

Finally, there are the 'developing

sources'. Joint venture deals are put in place, involving a tutelage programme, with these emerging suppliers. This is supported by the developed partners. The pay-off for their participation is access to low cost labour for time intensive production requirements. The system is held together through an expatriates programme where Nike personnel become permanent members of staff in each supplier's factory.

Unfortunately, there was a serious missing link. There had been insufficient consideration given to the employment practices of suppliers in some low cost locations. Accusations were made about exploitation of the emerging world. Global relationship management also calls for proper appreciation of ethical considerations.

number of companies for preferred supplier status. Although purchasing organizations often use different names for this approach, a significant number have pursued this type of consolidation process with notable success. For example, when Toyota made a strategic decision to invest heavily in motor manufacture in the UK, it focused on its potential supplier network several years ahead of components actually being required for volume car production. In line with best automotive practice, it applied very structured assessment of:

- supplier quality and delivery performance;
- cost drivers and price performance;
- technological expertise;
- and, most importantly, their preferred suppliers' management styles, commitment and capability.

Furthermore, through joint investment and close involvement with these companies during the start-up phase, it achieved improved and open business relationships, significantly reduced defects and cycle times, and stimulated much faster new product introduction times.

Partial adoption of collaboration

'At the beginning of the program, we identify functional and financial targets, and we cascade them down as we go from the vehicle system to multiple systems, then sub-systems, then components. Depending on the total scope of the supplier's responsibility, that determines when we bring them into the process.' Rosco Nash, Director Advanced Vehicle Technology, Ford.

Having decided to concentrate on preferred suppliers, and having tested the quality and price performance in comparison with the best companies in the market place, it is a relatively straightforward step for an organization to select an even smaller group of suppliers from this cohort for co-development through performance partnership agreements. Similarly, potential partners may be located from companies with whom the purchasing organization has had no previous contact. Under such circumstances the criteria for selection, and the method of assessment, need to be significantly more robust.

Excellent examples can be seen in companies such as Motorola, Intel, Digital and Texas Instruments, where there has been major transformation in relationships between the semi-conductor suppliers and their customers. Such companies have pursued similar routes in terms of supplier rationalization, joint definition of improvement plans and priorities, the creation of joint purchaser–supplier fusion teams with specific improvement objectives, and a focus on maximizing strategic value within the context of total cost of acquisition. Significantly, in such companies, the direction and leadership have come from the top. Joint business steering teams are in place, with representatives being drawn from both companies and their suppliers.

Business-to-business relationships are dynamic, not fixed. They are pursued as a means to an end, and not the end itself. A small number are enduring. The majority are fragile. Evaluate them on a project by project basis and be ruthless in the assessment of their performance (and yours).

It can now be seen that purchaser–supplier relationships can have a dynamic quality about them. In the scenario described above, companies are moving through the continuum from open competition into an arrangement of greater collaboration. This is described graphically in Figure 4.3. However, it is worthwhile correcting a potentially serious misunderstanding about such relational strategies. An important element of the approach is the need for flexibility. Partnering is only one of a number of

Figure 4.3

The balance between competitive and collaborative sourcing depends on the market place and supplier capabilities

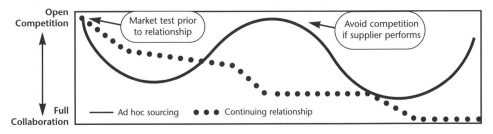

	COMPETITIVE SOURCING	COLLABORATIVE SOURCING
Beliefs	• Partnerships just lead to cosy relationships.	• Trust and openness prompt performance in return.
Purpose	• Use market pressure and available capacity to drive the best deal.	• Work together to create truly innovative and lean supply chain.
Expectations	• At some stage we will separate.	• We will be together a long time.
Pricing	• Price taker.	• Price maker.
Best Practice	• Competitive sourcing emphasizing pre-bid conditioning. • Performance contracting and imposed improvement goals. • Open book costing and full transparency.	• Principled approach to acceptable margins and return on investment. • Joint business development and co-marketing. • Sharing of risk and required investment.

approaches towards the management of the supply market. Most importantly, a number of preconditions and tests need to be applied to suppliers, and also the purchasing organization, if they are to succeed. In particular, there has to be:

'You must avoid the sin of naivety. It is important that the new enterprise should have no internal conflicts of interest.' Serge Tchuruk, Chairman, Alcatel-Alsthom, on the need to manage partnerships effectively.

- a commitment to openness on both sides and joint ways of working;
- a readiness to discuss future business plans and capital investment requirements;
- a preparedness to share each other's longer term strategies and business goals;
- a willingness to understand each other's business processes, managerial and operational cultures and their potential impact on the relationship;
- a strong sense of how the parties will mutually exploit a cost, quality, technical or marketing advantage via their collaboration;
- an agreed remedy in the event of a non-partnership source of greater advantage appearing in the supply market;
- a review forum capable of assessing how well the partnership has exploited or distorted the market to the advantages of both sides;
- a realistic assessment of the acceptability of the distribution of the benefits from the relationship between the partners.

A structured review of the nature of relationships between the parties benefits from an objective profile across a wide array of factors. An illustration of how a profile needs to be related to the different types of relational strategies is shown in Figure 4.4.

Clearly all of this has to be evaluated against potential developments elsewhere within increasingly competitive market places. Remember that relationships are dynamic, and will not necessarily endure beyond the specific goals of the defined project. But a central feature in the development of partnering is a preparedness on both sides to accept and support a process which explicitly maps out the required performance and obligations of the purchaser and

Figure 4.4

Business relationships can be competitive or collaborative. Either can be appropriate, depending on what you want to achieve

Relation-ship Factors	Profiling Key Factors in Supplier and Business Relationships		
	Free Market Competition	Mix of Competition and Collaboration	Full and Active Collaboration
Trust	Sufficient to meet operational requirements, e.g. quality or consistency.	Higher degree of trust and time commitment required.	Organizational interdependency calls for fundamental and total trust.
Existence of Common Goals	Irrelevant or not particularly important.	Not materially important, although there will be some overlap.	High correlation and overlap in terms of service, quality, technical innovation, time to market, cost drivers, environ-mental impact, etc.
Personal Relation-ships	May be helpful but not critical. If there are plans to move to a preferred status, relationships are likely to develop.	Positive relationships are likely to be found, within the frame-work of a preferred supplier agreement.	Relationships management may well be central to overall effectiveness. Detailed consideration will have been given to managing and building those relationships.
Continuity of Key Staff	Helpful for effective day to day purchasing, although not essential.	Provides a foundation for effective relationships, although not critical.	May well be the prime driver of the relationship. Change of senior people may lead to short term turbulence.
Required Compet-ence	Both parties must be committed to appropriate quality and competence of staff.	Suppliers likely to be selected on the basis of their competence and ability to add value over the medium term.	The possession of strategic competencies and capabilities may be at the heart of the relationship.
Expect-ations of the Parties	Delivery to specification leads to on-time payment.	Delivery to specification is enhanced over time by continuous improvement.	High levels of synergies and support to mutually extending expectations. Particularly noticeable in technology transfer, innovation flow and strategic cost management.
Internal Relation-ships	Likely to be at a fairly functional level.	On a regional or global basis, there will be defined access points between supplier and buyer.	Alliance selection will have been done at very senior levels. Alliance managers to liaise/ co-ordinate across transnational business groups.
Benefits for Each Party	Delivery to specification. Simple administration. On-time payment.	Closer relationship, clear direction, fair and reasonable treatment.	Mutually high expectations on profit, cost improvement, technical information, joint development programmes, etc.
Freedom to Switch Business	By definition, this will happen on quite a frequent basis.	Switching will be dependent on competitive performance and improvement potential.	Switching business would be as a result of a fundamental break-down in relationship.
Future Levels of Business	Will depend on circumstances in the market place.	Will depend on success of the relationship.	Jointly growing business may be a prime motivator.
Length of Relation-ship	Project by project in the short to medium term.	A minimum of one year plus.	Long-term investment and joint collaboration. Unlikely to be less than three years.

supplier. In addition, guiding principles need to be established on continuous improvement. Finally, both parties need to define an agreed process for evaluating the success of their agreement and the deliverables from it over a designated period of time. Not surprisingly, with such relationships we are invariably talking about single or reduced sourcing.

'This is a venture which was not invented in the boardroom but at the working level. We will not be reduced to silly games between the partners and we will not let egos get in the way.' Lou Noto, Chairman and CEO, Mobil, on the joint venture with BP to overhaul the European downstream oil industry.

The development and decline of relationships

Enduring success, however, can be quite fragile. Dedicated resources, from top management down, are usually required to sustain the relationship through the inevitable difficulties. Without such commitment there can be a high risk of the relationship quickly deteriorating and sliding back into a more exploitative and opportunistic mode of operation. Indeed, a most important perspective on the range of potential relationships available to organizations is that they should not necessarily be regarded as fixed. They can change over time. They are a means to an end, not an end in themselves. They can become closer, and they can also become more arm's length. After all, you may, or may not, have full control over them, depending on changes in the market place, regulatory controls, government intervention, changes at senior management level, changes in your own products or product technologies.

Furthermore, there are usually only a small number of suppliers who actually possess the required capabilities, resources and management commitment for you to consider a tied, longer term relationship. Indeed, a pervasive theme running through this analysis of the continuum of relational types, and the circumstances guiding their appropriate selection, is the need for clear and robust frameworks on how public or private sector organizations should analyse and map the business-to-business relationships that they require.

Unfortunately, there have been a number of celebrated failures in both product led and service delivery organizations as a result of misalignment between the strategic priorities of the various parties, the operational processes central to their achievement, and the preferred or imposed relational approach. The NHS case study from the UK is an unfortunate reminder of the disastrous consequences of selecting such a strategy without the necessary relational competence to support it. Detailed evaluation of a number of relational scenarios, and their implications, can facilitate more appropriate consideration of the most effective inter-

Selecting an appropriate relational strategy is not guesswork. It requires rigorous analysis and alignment of processes with required outcomes.

Case Study:
UK National Health Service
From collaboration to competition and back to (morale damaged) collaboration

The UK NHS spends over £40 billion each year. It is the second largest employer in the world, after the Indian State Railway. On a typical day in England, nearly 700,000 people will visit their doctor, 1.5 million items will be dispensed on prescription and 90,000 patients will be cared for at hospital outpatients' clinics. Since 1948, the NHS has provided comprehensive care; everyone in the UK has the right to use it, and it is provided according to clinical need not on a patient's ability to pay.

Traditionally, the system operated along collaborative lines. Indeed, there has been widespread praise for its cherished values of caring and open access. But there has also been much criticism of its bureaucracy, inability to develop preventive health strategy – it is really an 'ill health' service – and appropriation of power into the hands of the medical community. Political frustration led to the NHS and Community Care Act 1990 and the

introduction of an internal market. Money was to follow the patient. Health authorities and fundholding doctors were able to source healthcare from the most cost effective provider. In theory, competition between providers would force them to address structural weaknesses.

Alas, operationalization of the approach was poor. It relied on simplistic finance-based contracts with the occasional bit of quality thrown in. Transactional costs soared. Fragmentation of expenditure occurred, rather than much-needed consolidation and rationalization. Staff morale plummeted. A new Labour government in 1997 promised change.

The real need, however, is to address the crucial issue of the imbalance of supply of resources (which are capped) with demand for healthcare (which climbs inexorably). The prognosis for effective strategic prioritization in this area does not yet look particularly encouraging.

ventions. Such an approach helps address the confusion over the different options that are available and their suitability under a range of contingent circumstances.

Full and active collaboration

So far in this chapter the coverage has been primarily on purchaser–supplier product strategies in competitive or partially collaborative relationships. However, relational competence equally applies within downstream relationships involving, for example, distribution channels and also in the context of outsourced manufacturing. This may imply a somewhat restrictive view of the full potential of the approach. Organizations are not just sourcing, making or delivering products, they are actively competing over access to, and the development of, bundles of human skills, knowledge sets and capabilities which enable them to co-ordinate and integrate complex technologies and processes across a wide diversity of business activities and markets. These skills and capabilities are not necessarily product or function specific and, unlike products, they cannot easily be copied or duplicated. They are crucial in the creation and delivery of innovation.

As we saw in Chapter Three, it is possible to challenge many of the definitions involving the boundaries of business. Companies, and particularly the linked organizations with whom they have close and fully collaborative relationships, represent much more than just a mechanistic means of sourcing, producing and delivering products or services; they embody a cluster of interconnected and process specific capabilities. Defining, locating, assessing, acquiring, controlling, leveraging and protecting such capabilities is a crucial role for many organizations. As can be seen from the case study on SmithKline Beecham, collaborative access to such capabilities can become a prime route to achieving competitive advantage, providing it is possible to protect the intellectual property that will be generated from such alliances.

Case Study:
SmithKline Beecham
Strengthening market positioning through capability access in research

A major step in the transformation of SB through science-based innovation took place in May 1993, with the $125m alliance with Human Genome Sciences (HGS). The collaboration has produced the world's largest data base of human gene sequences, which has been thoroughly integrated into SB's discovery programmes. The company is now much better positioned than any competitor to take advantage of the revolutionary technology in genetic medicine.

SB's affiliation with HGS, in collaboration with the Institute for Genomic Research, is the largest among a growing number of scientific alliances which now complement SB's internal research capabilities. SB has established itself as 'partner of choice' in biotechnology, securing access to emerging technologies and products. Over the last three years, SB has entered into over 130 collaborations and agreements, including over 30 equity investments. In addition, more than 40 agreements with academia and bio-technology companies have strengthened leadership in the vaccine business.

This high level of activity illustrates SB's 'open door' policy to partnering – a prime way of achieving competitive advantage, through capability access and development, in the healthcare supply chain.

Clearly, if companies can achieve competitive advantage in this way, then it follows that they should concentrate on the identification and development of their capabilities within the context of access to third party expertise that complements their own skills. This broadens the definitions of relational competence far beyond traditional product specific and functionally led approaches that have so often dominated the supply chain.

A strategic, capabilities based definition of business-to-business relationships becomes a crucial lever for those companies determined to extend their market presence or pipeline of innovative products and services through joint development. This is invariably pursued through strategic alliances and co-ownership of equity in the associated ventures. It can now be seen that within the continuum of

Access to capability is becoming more important than merely sourcing a product or service. In turn, this requires a reevaluation of many of the methodologies being used to locate and assess potential suppliers.

Do you know the difference between the supplier base and the supply base? You are probably concentrating your attention on a restricted definition of third parties with the capabilities to meet your needs.

relational types, there needs to be an appropriate alignment between explicitly framed business needs, potential areas of risk and vulnerability, capabilities to be located, accessed or strengthened, and the required relationships to secure them with potential third parties. Unfortunately, as shown below, it is too easy to take a very narrow view of the market for the supply of such capabilities. In the example selected, it can be seen that when sourcing a product or service it is necessary not just to focus on the current or approved suppliers but to consider thoroughly the availability of all suppliers as well as those third parties who may possess the required processes and capabilities but who just happen not to supply the product at the current time.

Figure 4.5

Many companies are not aware of the total supply base. This chokes off available innovation and access to superior capabilities

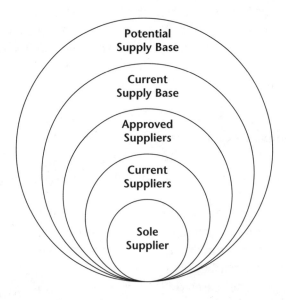

Assessing the required capabilities

It is now apparent that relational competence requires a structured assessment of three types of capabilities and their specific linkage to required business deliverables within the context of the supply market and the full range of contractual types. Such an assessment also facilitates considerably more balanced targeting and screening of potential trading partners. An example is provided in Figure 4.6 from the demanding area of strategic alliances.

■ **Secondary capabilities**: these normally refer to the capabilities which by their very nature are freely available within any market place. Such capabilities, and the products or services that are delivered through them, can be safely handled through shorter term contracts and relatively arm's length or competitive relationships.

Figure 4.6

A structured set of assessment criteria are used to narrow the field for a strategic alliance. Capabilities and compatibility are crucial

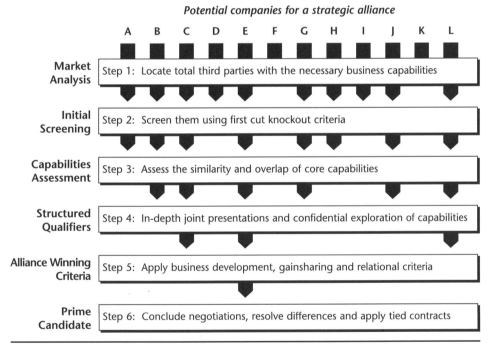

Potential companies for a strategic alliance

■ **Complementary capabilities**: are of much greater importance since they provide access to areas of expertise that will add significant value in the value proposition being delivered to end customers. They should normally be managed through more collaborative forms of contract and relational types, and over a longer period, than the less important secondary capabilities. They are prime targets for performance partnership and joint venture type arrangements.

- **Strategic capabilities** are normally associated with the close meshing in of business processes in successful strategic alliances or cross-shareholding. Of course, in many circumstances, their importance is such that they prompt one party to acquire the other. Prior to that happening it is essential that there is a fundamental alignment of business systems and processes between the parties. As was stressed in Chapter Three, it is crucial that these capabilities are properly protected in order for the competitive advantage that is being delivered through such sophisticated ways of working not to be eroded or diluted.

Broadening capability access through global sourcing

Just because global sourcing is theoretically possible does not mean that it is a sensible approach for your company. Local supplier development may be a much more effective option in value delivery than scouring every corner of the globe to find suppliers already capable of meeting your needs.

Global sourcing has become an important issue for many executives involved in supply chain transformation. It means locating and accessing supplier capabilities on a global basis and being prepared to source product or service against defined parameters such as cost, quality and service, without the use of intermediaries, while fully meeting internal organizational and production requirements. It involves the identification and management of new suppliers in multiple locations. It assumes that there is a competitive advantage to be gained by so doing, and that such sources are currently available.

It should be readily apparent that this approach is the exception rather than the rule for the vast majority of organizations. Few companies possess the resource or infrastructure to apply such a sourcing methodology. Admittedly a considerable number of companies do access international supply capabilities either via agents or through international purchasing offices. This is not global sourcing. Eight crucial questions need to be addressed.

- What are the complementary or strategic capabilities that need to be accessed in this way?
- Is global sourcing the most effective means of developing a competitive supply chain for your company?
- What additional deliverables will the global sourcing effort be expected to achieve?
- How is the potential global supply base structured to respond to such an effort?
- What risks and vulnerabilities will be encountered, and what is the probability of minimizing them to acceptable levels?
- How will investment in global supplier development be protected from access by your competitors?
- What are the organizational, resource and infrastructure implications of implementing global sourcing?
- Would it be more productive to focus effort on to developing the local or regional supply base?

It is clear that global sourcing should only be considered when addressing three prime requirements. Firstly, when your organization needs to access strategic capabilities that are either not currently available within your own region or where local capacity is severely constrained. Secondly, where the cost and quality advantages of global supply are such that it would place your business at a serious competitive disadvantage not to access supplier capabilities in this way. Thirdly, when a supply chain is concentrated in the hands of a small number of global players and where their market place power is being applied in a way that is unacceptable to your product and commercial objectives.

The opportunities from global sourcing are increasing dramatically in a number of sectors and, therefore, it should remain under close scrutiny by executives tasked with determining supply policy. But it needs to be approached with a full realization of the costs, resource demands and potential risks.

Developing relational competence action checklist

Activities to launch straight away

1. Identify the current level of relational competence within your organization.
2. Run workshops, briefing events, workshops and forums to build understanding of available approaches.
3. Segment products, services, supply chains and suppliers in line with the continuum of relational strategies.
4. Assess current vs. required levels of capability support in each area from external third parties.
5. Target a number of areas for performance improvement through greater use of free market competition.
6. Determine the opportunities for global sourcing in a small number of pilot project areas.
7. Locate initial suppliers capable of delivering a significant business advantage through global sourcing.

Initiatives to make a significant difference

1. Critically appraise the effectiveness of supply contracts, deliverables and relationships sourced within the competitive arena.
2. Form a supply improvement project team to determine the suppliers for relational development.
3. Frame systematic criteria, in capability terms, for the full range of relational types.
4. Assess the effectiveness of current relationships based around complementary and strategic capabilities.
5. Select the top priority areas for strategic alliances or similar high level relational initiatives. Define the process for their development in capability terms.
6. Ensure that rigorous assessment criteria are applied within strategic initiatives. Use them to monitor and support the relationships throughout their life cycle.
7. Extend global sourcing as a lever of change.

CHAPTER FIVE

Managing at the right level

Overview

1. Autonomy vs. collaboration in multi-site operations
2. Organizational control and process ownership
3. Dealing with the inefficiencies of decentralization
4. Assessing the scope for geographical consolidation
5. Capturing the synergies
6. Appropriate positioning of categories of expenditure
7. Role of informal networking and collaboration
8. Restructuring the intellectual services supply chain

The Bottom Line

While there are few genuine global businesses, determining the right level for control, ownership and delivery of supply chain processes raises organizational issues that need to be addressed in terms of appropriate geographical positioning. It is essential that there is an appropriate balance between autonomy, decentralization and empowerment and the necessary capture of cross-business synergies.

Think global – act local

'Much re-thinking is going on in the boardrooms of multinational companies, as the full impact of declining costs of transport and communication is felt and the old hierarchies of head office and subordinate regional outposts are dismantled in favour of greater local autonomy.' Helmut O. Maucher, Chairman of Nestlé SA, and President of the International Chamber of Commerce.

We are in an era when companies are expanding the geographical base of their operations. This is either being done organically, through acquisitions and mergers, or via trading connections such as strategic alliances and joint ventures. Indeed, some commentators are now arguing that the explosive growth of transnational alliances is signalling a fundamental change in the mode of organizing business activity. Furthermore, as was discussed in Chapter Two, national markets are increasingly losing meaning as the defining basis for the organization of some corporate led economic activity.

The emergence of a global economy, the development of networks of pan-regional linked businesses and the closer integration of supply chain working practices are challenging the organizational arrangements within which many local operating units deliver products and services to customers. There are many contradictory interpretations of what this means in practice. On the one hand, it is possible to regard the emerging global economy as a networked cluster of seamlessly integrated operations, connected through information systems and information technologies. Within such loose arrangements there is seen as being no role for conventional command and control practices, nor organizational hierarchy.

The counter-argument is less prosaic. Certainly we are dealing with organizational cultures that have embraced empowerment and devolved decision making. But the result is that within many medium sized to large organizations, in both the private and the public sector, there are invariably a number of individual businesses or groups of businesses that are operating autonomously. The result is often an uneasy relationship between centre and periphery. There can also be tension between country and regional groups. This is particularly the case in Europe and between Japan and certain south east Asian countries. The impact on day to day working operations can present a real challenge to supply chain professionals. Effective working practices, compatible standards and robust relationships are needed. As we can see from Figure 5.1, issues of control and ownership of processes at an appropriate geographical level have to be systematically addressed.

Figure 5.1

Organizational control and ownership of supply chain processes varies with appropriate geographical scale from local to global

Level of Geographical Aggregation		Examples of Supply Chain Processes and Control Points			
		Transactional Procedures	Supplier Management	Sourcing Strategies	Insource – Outsource
Local	Individual end user	◆	◆		
Local	Individual businesses	◆	◆		
Local	Country operation	◆	◆	◆	◆
Regional	Country cluster	◆			
Regional	Trading block		◆	◆	
Regional	Pan-regional		◆	◆	◆
Global	Regional clusters				◆
Global	Single hemisphere				
Global	Global		◆	◆	◆

◆ = Typical control points

Dealing with the inefficiencies of decentralization

One of the most powerful models of business management over the last 25 years has been that of 'small is beautiful'. Manufacturing companies have pursued this organizational and structural goal by splitting themselves into sectors, divisions, areas, countries, cost centres and strategic business units focused on particular product markets and customer groups.   Even when large organizations have grown outwardly bigger and broader through diversification and acquisition, they have tended internally to break themselves down into smaller and increasingly decentralized entities. Public sector bodies have adopted similar organizational strategies.   In the UK, examples can readily be seen with the emergence of agencies in government and hospital trusts in the healthcare sector.

'There is no global standard for management. We must tailor our approach to the situation.'
Nobuyuki Idei, President of Sony.

As we can see, though, from Figures 5.2 and 5.3, decentralization can also readily lead to a dependency upon local, country specific suppliers. While this may sometimes be appropriate, it is not always the most effective deployment of a company's total expenditure. It can result in:

■ erosion of total purchasing leverage with external suppliers;

■ different prices being charged in different markets for similar bought-in products and services;

■ differential pricing for identical products and services, from the same suppliers, in different countries;

Figure 5.2

Rationalization of supply and consolidation of expenditure may be undermined by local supplier dependency (real or perceived)

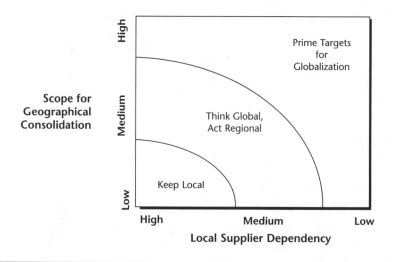

■ nationalistic sourcing, where local staff preference cuts across optimal supply configuration;

■ increase in business and transactional complexity resulting from a proliferation of local suppliers.

An assessment is needed of the potential for geographical consolidation and managing suppliers at the right level, across those categories of expenditure where local supply is not a prerequisite for product or service delivery to customers.

Clearly, the downside of decentralization is often very apparent within those organizations that are at an early stage in the development of integrated supply chain management. While there may be an apparent structural overlay of an above-country or cross-business supply organization, the reality is often that staff are overly focused locally on to meeting the pressing, operational needs of their sites and factories. Commercial advantage is traded off for service delivery.

When such an approach is well designed and competently managed it can lead to efficiency, close identification

Restructuring of organizations calls for consolidation of supply chain processes. This needs a determination to tackle the downsides of local business autonomy.

Figure 5.3

Determine which categories of expenditure and types of supplier should be managed locally, and which regionally or globally

Dependency on local supply network	Disagree ◄——► Agree
Assess the extent to which:	
1. There is strong business or functional preference for local supply.	1 2 3 4 5
2. There is considerable variance between country and regional specifications.	1 2 3 4 5
3. The category of expenditure is uniquely supplied to this business.	1 2 3 4 5
4. Local customers specify and/or directly manage the supply chain.	1 2 3 4 5
5. The local supplier has ownership of proprietary technologies, patents and property rights.	1 2 3 4 5

Scope for geographic consolidation	Disagree ◄——► Agree
Assess the extent to which:	
1. Suppliers operate on a regional or global basis.	1 2 3 4 5
2. There are few capability differences between local, country, regional and global suppliers.	1 2 3 4 5
3. There is little variance in specification across the business for the category.	1 2 3 4 5
4. There is commonality with other businesses over a specific category.	1 2 3 4 5
5. The product or service is managed across more than one business location	1 2 3 4 5

with the needs of the local market, development and support of a network of country specific processes and high levels of staff motivation and empowerment.

However, such a process can also be accompanied by either a hands-off attitude on the part of head office and corporate staffs, or an endorsement for loose networking arrangements to try and capture the synergies across the various locations. The participants in such cross-site collaboration processes, for example those involved in regional

'For a long time, we
had four separate
businesses,
pharmaceuticals,
consumer healthcare,
animal health and
clinical laboratories
each working in silos
independent of the
others. Developing
strategies of their own.'
Jan Leschly, CEO,
SmithKline Beecham,
on the need for
regional and global
integration of business
processes and shared
services.

purchasing councils or global commodity teams, often fail. They usually lack the necessary authority to act, while accountability for action is invariably unclear and indistinct. Local divisions and country specific businesses generally hold the power and narrow, parochial perspectives can easily prevail.

Capturing the synergies

Reliance on such a loose, network driven approach is inappropriate in most companies and requires significant strengthening.   This is the case in many transnational companies attempting to rationalize their supply lines in the context of realigning them with regional or global product manufacture. Geographical and process leverage of this kind is highlighted in Figure 5.4 and in the Bostrom and National Seating case study.   Equally, many similar

Figure 5.4

The process and deliverables from leveraging purchase expenditure at different geographical levels will usually vary significantly

	Local Networking	Country Leadership	Regional Centralization	Global Co-ordination
Executive Sponsorship	Not needed	General Manager	Regional President	Board Director
Focus of Activity	Tactical	Tactical, some strategic	Strategic, some tactical	Strategic
Cost Savings	Very low	Medium	Medium to high	Medium to high
Supply Performance Improvement	Medium	Can be high	Can be high	Medium
Organizational Complexity	Low	Low	Medium	High
Skills and Capabilities	Low	Medium	Medium to high	High
Best Practice Transfer	Usually non-existent	Often difficult	Needs a process	Often resisted

examples can be found throughout continental Europe, in the major business locations of Latin America, and across Asia Pacific country clusters such as Malaysia, Singapore and Indonesia, or India and Pakistan.

Case Study:

Bostrom and National Seating

Global collaboration: local delivery and adoption of best practice in lean supply

Far too many executives are inclined to believe that global collaboration and the application of leading edge manufacturing or commercial practice are only for the mega-corporations. Not so – as this case study neatly illustrates.

Bostrom is a UK vehicle seats maker with approximately half of its £85 million sales coming from the demand for heavy work vehicles such as tractors and excavators. It is a pioneering proponent of lean manufacturing techniques. National Seating is a US management buy-out company with sales of $70 million. Its centre for operations is in Knoxville, Tennessee, but it covers a wide geographical area through additional factories in Kentucky, Washington State, Virginia and Oklahoma.

It might be expected that the sales strategy would be marketing led, seeking to provide differentiated products to prime customers. In fact, neither company commands a huge amount of power in the market place.

Their market strength comes from three interlinked strategies. Firstly, they have decided to collaborate together with Bostrom taking a sizeable strategic stake in National Seating. This provides a platform for increasing sales through complementary synergies. Secondly, both companies are determined to improve their cost base. Headcount reduction is under way. Finally, they are applying lean thinking through simplification, rationalization and standardization of parts and working methods; revamping computer based stock control; and, most importantly, working with regional rather than country specific suppliers to switch to just-in-time rather than weekly deliveries. The enabling processes being adopted to facilitate all of this include giving greater freedom to act and accountability to smaller, self-managing teams. Also, Bostrom are committed to sharing and transferring their 'best manufacturing practices' to National Seating.

While it will take time to bring about the necessary changes, both businesses are totally committed to 'making change happen' through collaboration on lean supply.

The synergies and savings of supply chain consolidation are barely considered when targeting mergers and acquisitions. Calculate the potential earnings contribution. Then you will include this neglected area in your calculations.

Indeed, there is a groundswell of opinion that local business units and even operating divisions in many companies may provide too narrow a set of perspectives from which to make appropriate supply chain decisions. This can easily lead to serious neglect of the considerable opportunities that exist for pan-regional and global consolidation, particularly at a time when so many companies are involved in mergers and post-acquisition integration. Figure 5.5, for example, demonstrates the typical cost savings that can be readily achieved over a three year period through a concerted attempt to 'capture the synergies'.

Figure 5.5

Pan-regional and global consolidation of purchasing will deliver cost savings in excess of 20% through three phases of change

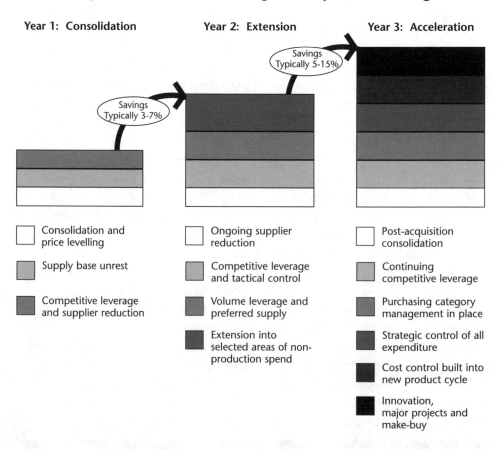

When challenging appropriate geographical positioning, it may be helpful to focus on a number of typical categories of expenditure.   An example drawn from a study for a European fast moving consumer goods company is shown in Figure 5.6. It can be seen how a number of categories are positioned at the wrong level. Too much sourcing had been done at the local or country level, rather than at the regional level. Furthermore, global synergies with their US parent company were not being harnessed.

Figure 5.6

Sourcing decisions should be taken at the highest possible geographical level to maximize leverage with suppliers

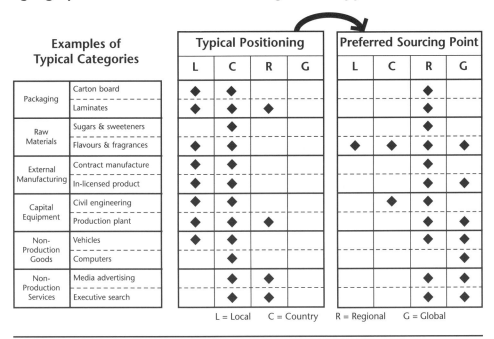

Examples of Typical Categories		Typical Positioning				Preferred Sourcing Point			
		L	C	R	G	L	C	R	G
Packaging	Carton board	◆	◆					◆	
	Laminates	◆	◆	◆				◆	
Raw Materials	Sugars & sweeteners		◆					◆	
	Flavours & fragrances	◆	◆			◆	◆	◆	◆
External Manufacturing	Contract manufacture	◆	◆					◆	
	In-licensed product	◆	◆					◆	◆
Capital Equipment	Civil engineering	◆	◆				◆	◆	
	Production plant	◆	◆	◆				◆	◆
Non-Production Goods	Vehicles	◆	◆					◆	◆
	Computers		◆						◆
Non-Production Services	Media advertising		◆	◆				◆	◆
	Executive search		◆	◆				◆	◆

L = Local   C = Country   R = Regional   G = Global

When an organization decides to embark on this type of assessment, then there are a number of typical questions that will need to be addressed.

- Is the internal supply organization operating at site rather than on a country, regional or global basis?
- How well is this internal structure functioning?
- What are the inefficiencies, expressed in financial terms, associated with the current approach?

- To what extent are suppliers organized on a similar geographical basis and where are customers located?
- Which suppliers have sufficient capability, and commitment, to supply regionally or globally?
- Which organizational processes need to be strengthened to ensure that knowledge and best practice can be successfully transferred from one country to another?

Balancing central control with decentralized collaboration enables a business to capture the benefits of centralization while leaving the responsibility and authority for day-to-day management of local suppliers with autonomous units. The challenge for executive managers is to work with their teams and create a process for the active sharing of knowledge and the co-ordination of concerted action across national and regional boundaries. By fully utilizing combined knowledge, total volumes and full bargaining power with suppliers, substantial profit improvement can be achieved. Introducing the approach usually leads to significant benefits for any business operating with decentralized operations, even when they are positioned across multiple market sectors. Furthermore, as well as reducing costs, the existing value delivery from suppliers, such as quality, service, innovation, technology transfer and customer support, can be appreciably enhanced. In addition, there is a valuable but less tangible organizational benefit; collaboration improves the overall effectiveness of business operations and strengthens team capability right across the company.

Local empowerment within a business framework

As we have seen in Chapter Four, in the context of global sourcing and market management, one way of capturing and leveraging shared knowledge is to set up a central function on a country, regional or global basis. This approach is particularly relevant in those sectors where suppliers and customers are also operating in a similar manner. The risk, however, is that central staff become isolated from the local business needs, or insufficiently responsive to market conditions.

An alternative approach is to adopt collaborative sourcing and networked market management. This secures the benefits of intra-business co-operation without imposing the disciplines of centralization. It allows greater professional freedom, while encouraging decentralized operating units to work together. However, as can be seen in Figure 5.7, a structured process for cross-business collaboration needs to be tailored to each business. While informal networking has a role to play, successful delivery

Figure 5.7

Informal networking and collaboration need to give way to more structured approaches to consolidation of the supply base

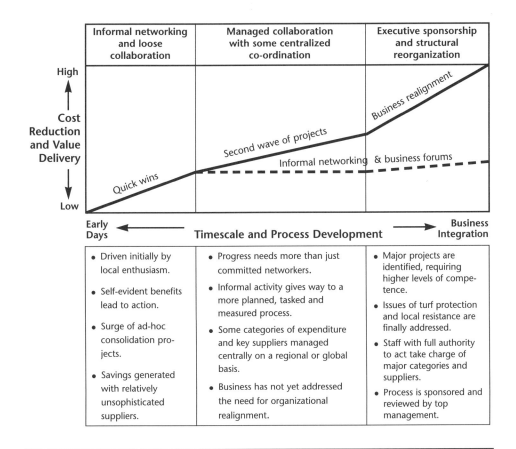

• Driven initially by local enthusiasm.	• Progress needs more than just committed networkers.	• Major projects are identified, requiring higher levels of competence.
• Self-evident benefits lead to action.	• Informal activity gives way to a more planned, tasked and measured process.	• Issues of turf protection and local resistance are finally addressed.
• Surge of ad-hoc consolidation projects.	• Some categories of expenditure and key suppliers managed centrally on a regional or global basis.	• Staff with full authority to act take charge of major categories and suppliers.
• Savings generated with relatively unsophisticated suppliers.	• Business has not yet addressed the need for organizational realignment.	• Process is sponsored and reviewed by top management.

Networking is a sub-optimal process, but a precondition to effective collaboration. It has to be strengthened by a defined way of working. There is a close correlation between the quantum of final deliverables and the level of active executive support.

of results requires an explicit and well structured implementation path. Unfortunately, a number of process issues are not always addressed effectively. Senior management needs to be prepared to invest time and resources in ensuring that:

- supply chain projects are being driven forward in response to valued business needs;
- expectations on outputs and results are explicit;
- a manageable and agreed number of projects are fully supported by top management of each operating unit;
- training and development is available to strengthen both individual and team capabilities.

This is the conclusion drawn from the Marley case study.

Case Study:
Marley USA
An executive led process in pan-regional purchasing collaboration

Many companies talk about leveraging the synergies across autonomous businesses, but fail to achieve them. Marley has succeeded in this by being able to develop a workable process for both cross-business and cross-functional collaboration.

Led by Larry Davis, President of Marley Mouldings, three businesses – General Shale, Marley Mouldings and Syroco – have put their purchasing power together and delivered impressive results to Marley plc, the parent company.

The key to success is full commitment and active co-ordination by Larry Davis, Dick Green and John Fravel, the Presidents of the three Marley divisions. At their quarterly meetings, collaboration projects are defined, prioritized and selected. A business mandate is

then developed within each division. Teams are selected to plan, organize and action a supply chain strategy incorporating the individual needs of each business.

Having developed the action plan, an explicit collaboration process is selected for each project. The members of all the businesses, working together, drive each project to completion. Progress is reviewed by the teams and top management at regular quarterly meetings.

This top down approach to collaboration has already delivered several million dollars of cost savings. Collaboration between autonomous businesses, that proactively manages the supply base, has become a way of life for Marley.

Restructuring the intellectual services supply chain

In every advanced economy, the share of the workforce employed in manufacturing has been falling for the past thirty years. For example, across the countries represented by the European Union it had dropped from 30% in 1970 to below 20% by 1996. In the USA the share had fallen from 28% to 15% over a similar period. Yet the majority of service industry supply chains, which dominate business today, have received scant attention in many instances.

Identify the very best practices that are being used in manufacturing supply. Target the interventions being used to transform value, cost and service delivery. Now benchmark intellectual services against them.

Indeed, even 'best practice' organizations are often inclined to perceive supply chain thinking as only being relevant for manufacturing assembly. Nothing could be further from the truth. This can be readily illustrated by examining the supply chain segment that covers intellectual services.

Accountants, lawyers, architects, consultants, creative media designers and analysts are significant employers, revenue generators, added value creators and opinion leaders around the world. There has been explosive growth in demand, as Figure 5.8 demonstrates for management consultancy. However, there has not been a parallel explosion in the most appropriate means of organizing their supply or managing their performance. The majority of intellectual service firms believe that they are offering high value, top level advice to their clients. Unfortunately many clients, by contrast, are increasingly sceptical of, and prepared to challenge, the nature of the value delivered and the costs associated with its provision. A number of traditional approaches to the procurement and delivery of such services need to be upgraded or replaced. In the face of changing client demands and accelerating competitive pressures, there will be a greater readiness to apply the supply chain tools and techniques that are to be found in manufacturing. Indeed, a number of trends can be detected in the conversion and application of such product related practices within a services context:

Figure 5.8

There has been huge growth in intellectual services supply. It has not been matched by effective processes for managing delivery

Growth of Management Consultancy

The Top Earners	Revenues 1995	Growth (%) Over 1994	No. of Consultants
Andersen Consulting	$4.2 bn	22	40,000
McKinsey & Co.	$1.8 bn	20	3,650
Ernst & Young	$1.5 bn	9	9,419
KPMG	$1.5 bn	28	8,915
Deloitte & Touche	$1.4 bn	20	6,000
Coopers & Lybrand	$1.2 bn	34	9,000
Mercer	$1.0 bn	13	8,900
Price Waterhouse	$1.0 bn	26	5,201
Booz Allen & Hamilton	$785 m	30	5,200
A.T. Kearney	650 m	19	2,700
Boston Consulting Group	$550 m	28	1,320
Gemini Consulting	$548 m	(1)	1,400
Arthur D. Little	$514 m	20	3,000+
Bain & Co.	$375 m	25	1,200
CSC Index	$200 m	14	450

With full acknowledgement to Worldlink of the World Economic Forum

- Traditionally, consultancy is a very fragmented sector.
- But, increasingly, consolidation is taking place with the barriers breaking down between lawyers, auditors, accountants and consultants.
- The major players are swapping local markets for global practices majoring on:
  - management of entire business processes;
  - acquisition integration and strategy competencies;
  - operational implementation of these strategies.
- They all need reference sites as demonstrators for clients.
- Huge gaps exist in transparency, performance contracting and incentivization.

- geographical consolidation and rationalization of the points of purchase;
- managing suppliers at a higher geographical level;
- the framing of company-wide guidelines on the sourcing of intellectual service providers;
- greater definition of the services to be purchased on a central basis but delivered globally or regionally;
- systematic evaluation of the future capabilities required in service provision, particularly in terms of information technology and knowledge transfer;
- more thorough framing of specific terms of engagement that set out roles, responsibilities, quality standards and required ways of working;
- development of charging structures that cover the delivery of defined performance and the transactional nature of the workload, e.g. differential payment to reflect value added, technical difficulty and importance of the work;

'What we want to ensure is that the law firm gravy train of the late 1980s doesn't come back.' Tim Clement-Jones, former Legal Director of Grand Metropolitan Retailing.

- much closer and more collaborative links between advisers and their clients in order to minimize duplication of time and effort;
- greater determination to conduct performance reviews and share best practice.

The Barclays case is a good example of a typical initiative from the legal area. It is applicable in many sectors.

Case Study:
Barclays
Realigning legal services through relational management

There are many hallowed grounds and cherished gardens in the professional services supply chain. Few dare tread in the comfortable and clubby world of consultancy, M&A, audit and legal services supply.

A notable exception has been Howard Trust, ex-legal director for BZW, and since 1995 group general counsel of the Barclays group of banking businesses. He quickly identified a number of features common to many areas of intellectual supply:

1. No knowledge of how much is spent on the service; with whom; and to what level of service quality.
2. No coherent, well defined and robust approach to the management of risk.
3. Internal isolation of specialist legal staff; lack of consideration about the most effective means of utilizing expertise centrally and across the business; external arrogance from suppliers keen to maintain the status quo.
4. Fragmentation of both internal and external supply, and no definition of preferred ways of working.

With legal expenditure running at £30 - £40 million a year, and with over 600 law firms involved around the world, a new legal framework was badly needed. Internal changes were made; the structure was decentralized; external law firms were reduced and realigned on a product basis. The same lawyers now provide advice on the same subjects but to many different businesses worldwide.

Identifying law firms most suited to the required way of working was effected through the joint production of 'relationship statements'. Those aligned to Barclays' needs have been very successful in the process. Twelve firms now account for 50% of the total expenditure, with almost 100 firms covering the rest.

The intellectual services world is not used to rationalization. It increasingly will be.

Managing at the right level action checklist

Activities to launch straight away

1. Map your current production based supply chain processes at a local and country level of operation.
2. Organize networking events, workshops, away days and review groups to foster close personal and working relationships between supply chain specialists.
3. Select a small number of cross-country, multi-site supply chain processes that could be enhanced through the adoption of a single, standardized approach.
4. Use project teams to map out, and implement, the required improvements in these processes. Ensure that project completion will take less than twelve months.
5. Evaluate the learning and implications from these starter projects. Develop agreed guidelines, principles and protocols that balance decentralized operation, formal collaboration and central control.

Initiatives to make a significant difference

1. Repeat the mapping of supply chain processes but broaden the focus of geographical aggregation to include country clusters, trading blocks, and pan-regional or global operations.
2. Extend this analysis from the manufacturing led supply chain into the non-production and non-inventory related or services area.
3. Form a top level executive forum to determine which processes are to be managed at which levels. This will be integrated with other broader business strategies.
4. Allocate process redesign and implementation to board directors, country general managers or site management depending on the level of strategic impact.
5. Agree a rolling three-year plan together with the financial, organizational and team capability deliverables.

CHAPTER SIX

The responsive supply chain

Overview

1. Creating platforms of best practice
2. Operational improvement across the supply chain
3. Efficient consumer response
4. Streamlining logistics, distribution and cross-docking
5. Demand forecasting and planning
6. Time compression and lead time reduction
7. Synchronized production
8. Inventory management
9. Driving out complexity and supplier rationalization
10. Capability development in the supplier chain

The Bottom Line

In many business sectors there is an accelerating trend towards greater integration of supply chains in terms of demand and supply management. This is being driven by the need to respond quickly to the requirements of ever more demanding customers and consumers.

Towards customer responsiveness

There have been many significant developments over the past forty years in managing suppliers and the supply chain. In the 1960s the prevailing approach was on securing stability in production through modelling on economic batch quantities, safety stocks and reorder levels. This provided a natural platform for the adoption by many western companies of MRP in the 1970s and early 1980s. Figure 6.1 highlights the aims of such an approach. In

Figure 6.1

Innovation in the production supply chain builds on previous platforms of best practice. Many companies are still catching up

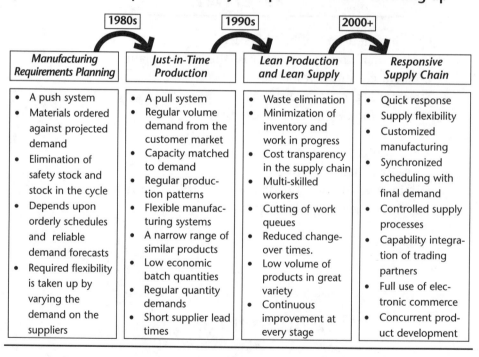

1980s	1990s		2000+
Manufacturing Requirements Planning	*Just-in-Time Production*	*Lean Production and Lean Supply*	*Responsive Supply Chain*
• A push system • Materials ordered against projected demand • Elimination of safety stock and stock in the cycle • Depends upon orderly schedules and reliable demand forecasts • Required flexibility is taken up by varying the demand on the suppliers	• A pull system • Regular volume demand from the customer market • Capacity matched to demand • Regular production patterns • Flexible manufacturing systems • A narrow range of similar products • Low economic batch quantities • Regular quantity demands • Short supplier lead times	• Waste elimination • Minimization of inventory and work in progress • Cost transparency in the supply chain • Multi-skilled workers • Cutting of work queues • Reduced change-over times. • Low volume of products in great variety • Continuous improvement at every stage	• Quick response • Supply flexibility • Customized manufacturing • Synchronized scheduling with final demand • Controlled supply processes • Capability integration of trading partners • Full use of electronic commerce • Concurrent product development

parallel, and particularly in eastern countries such as Japan, a different focus was emerging. Just-in-time (JIT) practices were evolving alongside total quality management (TQM), in a drive to eliminate waste from manufacturing operations. A mix of improvement interventions was adopted; neither JIT nor TQM were based on single techniques.

Indeed, it is more appropriate to regard them as business philosophies supported by a variety of interconnected activities and based around three core QCD principles; a continually improving quality assurance system to meet customer requirements, a continually improving cost management system to provide the product at an attractive price to the customer while securing reasonable profits for the company, and a continually improving delivery system to ensure that products arrived on time. As Figure 6.2 graphically illustrates, huge improvements are

'We were fairly arrogant, until we realized the Japanese were selling quality products for what it cost us to make them.' Paul A. Allaire, President, Xerox.

Figure 6.2

A huge amount of improvement remains to be achieved across the complete supply chain. Performance gaps of 50% are common

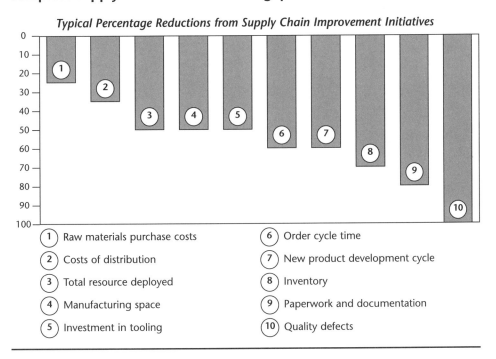

Typical Percentage Reductions from Supply Chain Improvement Initiatives

1. Raw materials purchase costs
2. Costs of distribution
3. Total resource deployed
4. Manufacturing space
5. Investment in tooling
6. Order cycle time
7. New product development cycle
8. Inventory
9. Paperwork and documentation
10. Quality defects

available in supply chain performance. However, without the integration of all three approaches in a system driven by *kaizen* (from the Japanese *kai*, meaning change, and *zen*, meaning good or for the better), there is a risk that quality and customer response would be traded off for cost savings.

'We have complicated our business out of sight and we're doing many things that do not add value.' Andy Robson, Head of Supply Chain Projects, Institute of Grocery Distribution.

By the mid-1980s, there was a growing acceptance that MRP and JIT, as separate processes, could co-exist. MRP became recognized for what it was designed to be – a priority scheduling system. It could not replace the need for shop floor control systems which eliminated time, waste and materials from the manufacturing environment. Thinking lean, getting lean and staying lean became a preoccupation as companies moved into the late 1980s' recession. Essentially, lean was a timely challenge to mass production thinking.

Figure 6.3

Audit how time is allocated in the supply chain. Assess where value is added. Then set the goals for change and improvement

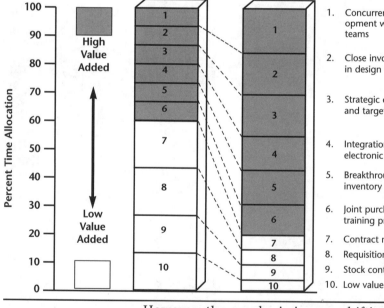

However, the emphasis is now shifting from one of eliminating waste within individual manufacturing entities to eliminating inefficiency from complete supply chains. The focus is increasingly on how companies can most effectively meet the needs of their demanding customers (such as retailers) and the ultra-value conscious end consumer. This calls for development of the responsive supply chain.

Operational improvement across the supply chain

Successful operational strategy calls for the development of a helicopter quality: the ability to view entire supply chain processes and structures at a glance and drill down on to what works and what needs improvement. All too frequently, prime opportunities are ignored by adopting a partial approach. It is easy to focus only on day-to-day operations and remain immersed in the detail of processing requisitions, expediting materials and managing crises. In this section, a number of areas for improvement are highlighted. It is by no means comprehensive but points out the scope for change. The goal is to achieve a step change in customer response, cost reduction and a dramatic conversion of under-utilized assets back into cash.

Efficient consumer response (ECR)

When Taiichi Ohno, then Toyota's chief engineer, visited the USA in the late 1940s, he was allegedly more impressed by the country's supermarkets than by its auto industry. Their approach to logistics and stock replenishment inspired his development of just-in-time production. Fifty years on, retailers are increasingly applying their own version of JIT. Efficient consumer response employs a number of already well known, if insufficiently practised, concepts and tools in supply chain management. Most importantly, it requires an integrated approach in terms of:

- automated store ordering via point of sale scanning;
- retailers sharing live sales data on line with suppliers;
- joint development and integration of compatible computer systems;
- suppliers and retailers working closely together on planning and demand forecasting;
- efficient scheduling and operation of product introductions, promotions and assortments;
- co-managed inventory, with suppliers taking over responsibility for replenishment;

'The revolution today is the development of value retailing and the focus on price. There is an inexorable move to more efficient forms of retailing. It's not flair that's going to win the day – too many people have got that now. What is critical is greater efficiency in delivering the product to the customer.' George Willace, CEO of retail analysts Management Horizons.

- cross-docking with manufactured products combined and consolidated with other suppliers' products destined for the same retailer;
- 100% on-time, in full delivery with 100% correct orders;
- automatic electronic funds transfer.

'We have to move from a 'push' approach, which relies on putting products in a warehouse and hoping they will sell, to one where the industry is pulled forward by consumer demand.' Phil Marineau, President, Quaker Oats.

Without any doubt there are huge potential cost savings, and dramatic improvements in customer response, to be obtained through such supply chain collaboration. Indeed, according to the ECR Europe Executive Board, a group of manufacturers, retailers and consultants interested in the approach, $27 billion a year could be cut from the cost of Europe's food retailing industry through more effective management of the supply chain. Inventories would drop by more than 40%, and operating costs by 4.8%.

Finally, it is worth emphasizing that 25% of the supply chain costs can be incurred in the final hundred yards of the chain from the back of a store to the shelves and onwards to checkout. Information technology is a powerful enabler of change in this area. Electronic point of sale systems speed up check-out lanes; self-service scanners and electronic price tags can eliminate queues; electronic shelf-edge labelling provides accurate pricing information for customers; data warehouses profile customers and demand patterns; and electronic data interchange can transmit relevant data instantaneously between trading partners.

Centralized distribution centres and cross-docking

Over the past decade there has been a significant move to centralizing distribution centres and applying cross-docking. In the past many manufacturers delivered direct to the depots or outlets of their retail customers. Such operations were push systems, driven by the supplier. Deliveries are now increasingly made to a central distribution point run by the retailer, or by a contractor working on behalf of the retailer, who then controls final distribution through to the stores. Substantial emphasis is placed on the use of information technology and supply modelling software to ensure optimal vehicle loading, route planning and scheduling. The goal is store replenishment in less than eight hours with deliveries arriving within thirty minutes of specified times. The extensive rationalization at ICA in Sweden demonstrates the improvement in customer responsiveness and profit margins that can be secured. Cross-docking has been integrated within this approach. It involves the receipt of full pallet loads of goods and then the shipping of these same pallets, or loads composed of

It is the business-to-business hostility that creates supply chain waste. Convert this into a relational advantage. Be the leader that triggers a different way of working.

Case Study:

ICA

Cutting retail costs by 50% through rationalization of distribution

At the end of the 1980s, the Swedish retail market was suffering from recession, deregulation prior to joining the European Union, and accelerating price competition between the major players. Profit margins at their leading retailer – ICA, with a third of the grocery market – were being eroded further by a highly efficient internal supply chain. A multi-divisional structure, separate supply and distribution systems and non-integrated marketing strategies added plenty of cost but insufficient value.

Throughout the past six years, however, this position has been transformed. In particular, logistics costs have been halved. How?

1. Rationalization of the divisional structure into wholesale and retail operations.
2. Closure of over 50% of their regional distribution centres. Introduction of three cross-docking centres.
3. Introduction of a 'back-bone' communications network to integrate and link 2,700 stores with the group's commercial and marketing operations.
4. Product needs channelled electronically to common distribution points and then on to suppliers.
5. Daily rather than weekly deliveries. 50% reduction in inventories held in the supply chain.
6. Additional synergies obtained by using the network to transfer marketing information, performance data, pricing analyses and training material between the participants.

Such transformational restructuring of the cost base has required persistent endeavour and top management commitment to succeed. This is a consistent key to success.

sorted pallets from different suppliers, without any of the goods being packed away. This can dramatically reduce handling, storage and labour costs, through the elimination of put-away and order picking. Successful implementation is achieved through:

- close involvement of suppliers and the customer in developing an effective process, one that minimizes the risk of simply shunting costs from one party to another;
- effective part and product identification and seamless communication across the cross-docking operation;
- timely electronic supply of reliable information on both incoming and outgoing shipments;
- tracking and managing actual and projected workloads, especially at peak times.

The essence of the quick response approach is no longer about selling what you buy, but about buying what you sell.

Demand forecasting and planning

Almost all organizations have some form of system for forecasting customer demand, since it is a crucial input into planning materials, manufacturing, distribution and capacity loading. The trouble is that most companies are modelling production on inaccurate, doubtful forecasts. The basis of such systems is usually a combination of statistical forecasts based on historic usage and market intelligence provided by sales and marketing. There is often a low level of input from the customer. Encouragingly, two changes are under way:

- a readiness to harness the potential of sophisticated quantitative modelling techniques to provide more accurate and stable forecasts;
- access to point-of-sale data to eliminate the demand distortion which results from ordering and backlog clearance patterns at higher levels in the supply chain.

However, the sharing and reconciliation of short and long - term demand forecasts between trading partners is still rare. This is the major barrier to improving forecasting effectiveness, but one that was effectively tackled within Carl Karcher Enterprises.

Case Study:

Carl Karcher Enterprises

A meaty performance through demand and supply integration

Carl's Jr., renowned for hamburgers, knows how to ensure when the time is right to order buns, frozen beef patties and tomatoes.

Since 1993, Carl's Restaurants in the western USA and Mexico have controlled 677 outlets through a computer based demand management system. Through two distribution centres, in Anaheim and Manteca, California, it is able to keep the goods flowing.

Carl's Jr. developed a strategic initiative to ensure that the right items, in the right quantities, arrived in the right locations by integrating forecasting and inventory management, with frozen meat, perishable produce and limited shelf life items. This integration of demand and supply was a critical pathway to success.

Since the initiative, and installation of the computer system, Carl's Jr. has reduced inventory from $4.7 million to $3.2 million. Stock outs have been improved by 34% and inventory turns are now running at 64 times a year.

Time compression and lead time reduction

Management of time across the supply chain is a strategic issue for many businesses. While tactical lead time reduction has been quite common, a lead time being the interval between an event being scheduled and its occurrence, it has tended to be applied piecemeal. A total improvement in speed of response, particularly in product development, manufacturing cycle time and inventory management, will generate significant benefits in both working capital and assets utilization as well as through revenue generation. Areas to target include:

The goal should be to achieve a reliable process capable of cutting new product development time by at least 50%. This requires concurrence between product design, manufacturing process development, purchasing, suppliers and marketing.

- concurrent vs. sequential new product development;
- measuring and reviewing throughput and time efficiency (actual vs. optimal);
- application of design for manufacturability;
- reduction of supplier delivery and in-house flow times;
- abandonment of complex matrix structures and reduction in hierarchical ways of working;

- integration of flows of information and goods across the complete supply chain;
- defining the interfaces at each stage in the chain;
- defining and attaching a time value to the overall costs of design and development;
- introduction of electronic commerce, electronic data interchange and bar coding to speed up material flows.

Synchronized production

'We've moved away from banging out products at high volume to asking customers what they want and operating plant flexibility.' Tony Ward, Operating Director, Renold.

This involves producing components or products at a rate which matches customer demand. It is achieved through applying short manufacturing lead times and supplying against actual needs. It calls for very short-term forecasts with high accuracy levels. The way in which this is achieved varies with the different types of production processes, but usually involves:

- investment in 'flexible' manufacturing equipment;
- redesigning business processes around a 'pull system' that maximizes such manufacturing capabilities;
- shifting the emphasis from fixed quality variable sequence to variable quality fixed sequence production;
- off-line set-ups on tooling and improved process reliability;
- reviewing design tolerances which impact running speeds or reject rates;
- improving the availability of materials or components used in the manufacturing process;
- manufacturing improvement teams dedicated to process analysis, identification of opportunities and project management of the required process improvements.

Supplier rationalization

A number of organizations and academics have portrayed supplier rationalization as a goal to be pursued in its own right and as an end in itself. This is incorrect. It confuses ends and means. Reduction in the number of suppliers should result from implementing a specific supply chain strategy, or be one of the enablers in achieving it. We saw in Chapter Four that delivery of appropriate value to customers may require closer working relationships between trading partners. Time and resource inputs by the various parties to achieve that goal will be high. This may mean, by necessity, that required focus, commitment and deliverables can only be achieved by working with a reduced number of suppliers. This was the approach adopted by Quaker Oats and described in the case study. A decision on how many suppliers a business requires to meet its defined goals should be framed within that context and not by reference to arbitrary or notional targets. Factors to be taken into account include:

Be very wary of fixed targets for supplier reduction. You require an appropriate number that meets your customer, production and financial needs. That is also defined within a systematic assessment of potential risk.

- the power in relational terms between purchaser and suppliers, resulting from the chosen strategy;

Case Study:

Quaker Oats Company

Rationalizing, restructuring and integrating the packaging supply chain

In rationalizing its folding carton supply chain, Quaker Oats reduced its supply base from twenty-one suppliers to just two. One of these, Field Container of Elk Grove, Illinois, is now one of their strategic suppliers for breakfast cereal containers.

Quaker Oats, seeking to create efficiency in its planning and supply process, had been searching for a true alliance partner; one capable of participating in the planning process for folding cartons. This relationship is now structured in a way which creates efficiency for both firms. Furthermore, Field has a long-term commitment from Quaker and is investing to ensure a successful alliance.

Field has co-located Partnership Manager Jim Brown at Quaker Oats;

purchased several million dollars of capital equipment; dedicated a production line to Quaker Oats and streamlined the manufacturing process. Production schedules are transmitted and produced daily, greatly reducing inventory and staff costs. Quaker Oats have reduced inventories from six months to just under one month.

This programme capitalizes on Field's vertical integration and enables the parties to achieve lowest cost status throughout the supply chain and, in turn, a sectoral competitive advantage.

When companies form open, transparent, strong relationships, dedicated focus, integrated strategies and a commitment to lowest cost, efficiency and high productivity, supply chain management is maximized.

- information technology and other investment costs associated with single, dual and multiple sourcing;
- a market assessment of future supplier capacity;
- the staff resources required and available to build and manage appropriate supplier relationships;
- the staff resources required to implement purchaser–supplier improvement projects;
- the time and cost of exit strategies in the event of non-performance;
- risk assessment of market place, technology and financial factors;
- the likelihood of the parties failing to commit appropriate investment to sustain technology performance and competitive advantage;
- cost and price benefits from volume consolidation;
- the impact of diluting or losing competitive leverage.

Automatic inventory replenishment (AIR)

This approach to inventory management is used predominantly for multiple use, low value items in a manufacturing environment and for engineering spares. The aim is to improve efficiency in the ordering and replenishment process and provide the supplier with more freedom to respond directly to the purchaser's requirements. Both parties agree the delivery quantities for a particular item and a fixed stock location is allocated. Two bags, each containing the delivery quantity, are placed in each stock bin. When production requires more of an item, one bag is issued. The supplier checks the purchaser's stock locations on a frequent basis, replenishes the bags and invoices electronically for the items supplied. As soon as the bin is replenished, the stock becomes the property of the purchaser.

Potentially, the approach is subject to abuse and a fair level of trust is required between the parties. The challenge is then to secure the right balance between control and efficiency from the purchaser's perspective and freedom to act for the supplier.

Consignment stocking

In this arrangement, stock is owned by the supplier but held at the purchaser's site of use. Responsibility for forecasting demand and replenishing the stock to agreed levels rests with the supplier. The system requires open access, ready contact and preparedness to share information. It provides three main advantages to the purchasing organization: lower stock levels, reduced risk of stockouts, and extended payment terms.

Inventory management is about optimizing the balance between the costs of supply, the costs of production, the costs of stock holding and the need to provide the highest level of service to customers. Few corporations have got this balance right. Change and improvement come as much from the development of different types of commercial relationship with trading partners as they do from the technologies of co-managed inventory and efficient replenishment.

Suppliers benefit through more aligned and responsive production, together with direct monitoring of consumption. When considering the introduction of consignment stock, there is a need to underpin the arrangement with a tailored agreement that reflects the capabilities of both parties, the nature of their relationship and the expenditure categories to be supplied. This will reflect:

- definitions of the product, together with health, safety and environmental considerations;
- responsibilities for data provision, forecasting, replenishment and physical storage;
- minimum and maximum stock levels;
- the replenishment cycle;
- rules for segmentation of stock and passing of property;
- stock accuracy targets and estimated annual usage;
- circumstances under which the supplier can withdraw stock for use elsewhere;
- invoicing and payment;
- remedies if either party fails to perform.

Supplier managed inventory (SMI)

This builds on the consignment stock approach through closer integration between the parties. While consignment stocking is usually introduced by the purchaser, elements of SMI may be initiated by the supplier. There has been considerable interest in the approach, especially between first tier suppliers, retailers and distributors.

Managing the movement of the product is a crucial consideration with a number of options available including:

- third party distribution organized by the purchaser, utilizing the third party's assets;
- third party distribution utilizing vehicles and equipment owned by the purchaser;
- third party distribution utilizing vehicles and equipment leased by the purchaser;
- third party distribution organized by the supplier;
- distribution managed by the supplier using own assets;
- distribution managed by the purchaser using own assets.

Decisions on which options to choose involve:

- the respective power of the purchaser and supplier;
- the power a third party acquires in the process;
- the ease of switching third party distributors;
- the size and frequency of the required deliveries;
- the total cost of each item.

Streamlined logistics and distribution

The emphasis throughout logistical improvement should be on throughput and flow as much as on storage. Streamlining distribution rapidly takes you into customer responsiveness. You will then have to be prepared to re-think the supply chain completely.

Logistics is all about managing the flow of materials and information from source to customer across the entire range of materials handling and movement functions and throughout an organization and its supply channels. It has a huge impact on the deployment of assets since all goods in transit are major consumers of capital resources. This was certainly the conclusion drawn by United Biscuits. Unfortunately, there is an enormous gap between best practice and the average performers in this area. In many companies there is still a need to shift from a warehousing approach, centred around storage, to a much greater emphasis on managing and accelerating material flow. This forces the necessary focus on customer responsiveness, speed of operation and streamlining the total process. Indeed, it can prompt a complete redefinition of the supply chain. A number of more specific areas to address include:

- improved delivery planning, scheduling and tracking of consignments;
- flexible routing and more efficient vehicle loading and unloading;
- assessing the appropriate mix of in-house and third party distributors against defined criteria;

Case Study:
United Biscuits
Flexibility and quick response drive a successful cost avoidance exercise

In the late 1980s, United Biscuits predicted that retail trends in the UK would require lower inventories and more frequent deliveries from suppliers. In response, they decided to tackle warehousing and distribution as an exercise in strategic response and cost avoidance.

At that time stock was held in six bulk warehouses and up to 28 secondary depots. Despite almost a 100% increase in stock keeping units (SKUs), they now operate with one warehouse and six distribution centres. Average stock turns on warehousing of seven days have been achieved, against their target of 10-12 days. By pulling stock in from the manufacturing sites, they are able to offer totally consoli-dated orders to supermarkets.

Success has been achieved through a combination of activities. Responsiveness and flexibility was the key theme. There was a recognition that distribution systems were about quick response and not merely about storage. On the warehousing side, there are now fewer loading bays, discouraging excess storage and stock assembly. Productivity initiatives have focused on ways of keeping the product moving.

Despite considerable success, there is full recognition that supermarket customers will continue to demand increasingly higher levels of response performance. This remains the driver and focus of future initiatives.

- application of decision support systems with respect to markets, products, service levels, route planning, vehicle tracking and systems connectivity;
- reviewing transit times and intermediate stock holding;
- local customization, i.e. adding value to the product at the last moment in the supply chain.

In major companies the concept of focusing on the integration of logistics across entire regions is rapidly taking hold. Increasingly, this involves the replacement of local and national warehouses and associated distribution arrangements with pan-regional, single hubs.

Improved warehousing practice

While working with suppliers to eliminate inventory and improve efficiency is a key feature of responsive supply, it is equally important to ensure that the stock holding capabilities of the purchasing organization are not ignored:

- monitor and control closely the complete process of goods reception, storage, picking and despatch to achieve maximum cost effectiveness;
- thoroughly understand longer term needs of customers and plan warehousing improvement accordingly;
- make sure that material flow and information flow are aligned. Strengthen stock data monitoring, measurement and feedback;
- avoid warehousing solutions which require excessive racking and space for kitting or load assembly;
- ensure that the goods are kept moving between receipt and storage, and adopt a continuous improvement mentality.

Finally, it is worth noting the experiments under way with 'virtual warehousing' in regions where goods need to cross several countries. Plans are in place, particularly in Europe, to cut the cost of importing through one-off co-ordination of customs tariffs. Centralization and harmonization of this kind would avoid the need to respond to the wide array of cross-border regulations, valuations and exchange rates that are currently encountered.

Driving out complexity in purchasing

In Figure 6.4, a wide array of initiatives have been summarized. All of them can be applied across the supply chain as part of a planned campaign to drive out complexity. One particular strand of such a programme, the rationalization of low value purchasing, is described below.

Figure 6.4

Simplicity pays off across the supply chain. There is still a need to launch and sustain initiatives that drive out complexity

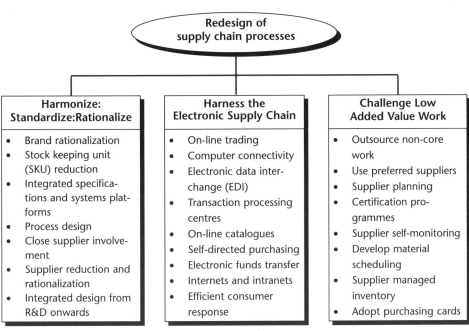

Harmonize: Standardize:Rationalize	Harness the Electronic Supply Chain	Challenge Low Added Value Work
• Brand rationalization • Stock keeping unit (SKU) reduction • Integrated specifications and systems platforms • Process design • Close supplier involvement • Supplier reduction and rationalization • Integrated design from R&D onwards	• On-line trading • Computer connectivity • Electronic data interchange (EDI) • Transaction processing centres • On-line catalogues • Self-directed purchasing • Electronic funds transfer • Internets and intranets • Efficient consumer response	• Outsource non-core work • Use preferred suppliers • Supplier planning • Certification programmes • Supplier self-monitoring • Develop material scheduling • Supplier managed inventory • Adopt purchasing cards

Low value items are a classic example of the 80:20 Pareto principle. The 'trivial many' over-dominate the 'vital few' in terms of the utilization of staff resource and administrative procedure. In many organizations 80% of purchase categories and suppliers represent less than 20% of the total expenditure. Commit to an ongoing campaign to reduce needless complexity in this area:

- identify the low value purchase categories such as office supplies and MRO items;
- standardize, harmonize, rationalize and consolidate wherever possible;
- introduce purchasing cards (an example is provided from a UK Government initiative);
- group items into category clusters, increase volume leverage, negotiate with suppliers, streamline the delivery systems, simplify requisitioning and payment;
- introduce preferred supplier schemes;

'The real question is whether you can put the right paradigm in place, so the process has fewer moving parts and less things to break down. It's very important to change the process fundamentally. You need to change the whole behaviour of the company, to become more responsive to the customer.' Denis Nayden, President of GE Capital.

- adopt blanket orders and systems contracts whereby a supplier is selected to deliver goods on receipt of an authorized release from a purchaser;
- introduce electronic trading, self-directed purchasing via on-line catalogues and centralized transaction processing centres;
- outsource back-room and minor service functions including low value purchasing.

Case Study:
UK Government
Cutting back on paperwork and processing costs

The National Audit Office, the UK government's spending watchdog, had been critical for some time of the inefficiencies and transaction costs for low value purchasing. In one study of the Ministry of Defence they found that it cost £70 in administration for every order handled – including one for items costing just 98 pence.

After interminable debate, the British government finally caught up with the private sector and decided to introduce up to 100,000 purchasing cards to pay for goods such as stationery and office equipment. It is estimated that this will save between £60 and £100 million every year.

But the big gain will be in refocusing staff effort on to higher value activity.

'What we see is that people involved in the paper chase will be freed up to spend more time getting better deals.' Geoffrey Robinson, Paymaster-General, UK Government.

Capability development in the supplier chain

Many manufacturers involved in implementing supply chain integration programmes have focused primarily on a number of linked interventions:

- reviewing supplier selection criteria to pinpoint requirements for supplier improvement programmes and/or removal of poorly performing suppliers;
- redefining selection criteria to assess both capabilities in product manufacture and relationship management;
- implementing supplier audits, supplier certification programmes, tracking and reporting procedures;
- increased purchaser–supplier interaction via supplier associations, supply clubs, technical residencies, forums and feedback sessions;

■ greater and earlier supplier involvement in product design and new product development.

All of these approaches have been designed to develop a more responsive supplier chain and strengthen supply capabilities. Leading edge manufacturers, such as Black & Decker, have now added supplier training and development to their improvement programmes. This is designed to enhance their supply chains for the future. A number of companies, such as Boeing, Digital, Motorola and Xerox, have gone beyond this stage and joined forces in a consortium designed to co-ordinate capability development through supplier training centres (STCs) at community colleges and universities. These centres offer an integrated programme including needs assessment, direct training and follow-up reinforcement on subjects such as ISO9000, cycle time management, design for manufacturability and six sigma quality processes.

'The three most important requirements for kaizen are one, top management commitment, two, top management commitment, three, top management commitment.'
Masaaki Imai, Founder of the Kaizen Institute.

Case Study:
Black & Decker
Joint training of first line managers with key supplier companies

Spennymoor in England is Black & Decker's largest manufacturing plant for its international operations. It exports well over 70% of its annual output. Pressures of global competition have made the company push continually to improve quality, efficiency and productivity.

As part of a programme of work based training they decided to extend the development of first line managers into their key suppliers. This was organized fortnightly over a 15 month period and was supported by open learning modules, coaching, work based activities and projects.

A steering group of senior managers from the companies met monthly to ensure that the programme was meeting the defined objectives of better customer–supplier relationships, significantly fewer defects and faster new product introduction times. In turn, each supplier launched its own internal development programme.

Deliverables from the projects were particularly impressive with measurable improvements in packaging, delivery systems, stocking systems and product development as well as significant cost savings.

The responsive supply chain action checklist

Activities to launch straight away

1. Set immediate short-term goals for inventory reduction. Locate the principal bottleneck areas and target them for improvement.
2. Review and develop more appropriate supplier selection criteria and apply them to supply rationalization and assessment.
3. Locate a number of pilot project areas for greater involvement of suppliers in new product development.
4. Experiment with alternative forms of inventory management with suppliers accepting greater responsibility for replenishment.
5. Set up joint purchaser–supplier training programmes.
6. Launch a complexity reduction programme across low value purchasing.

Initiatives to make a significant difference

1. Calculate the true costs of inventory and time across the supply chain in terms of capital efficiency and asset utilization.
2. Challenge the roles of functions and interfaces between different departments. Transfer staff to multi-process, multi-functional project teams.
3. Map the processes and sub-processes of the supply chain and radically rethink every aspect of its operation.
4. Address the crucial issue of two-way flows of information between trading partners and the required commercial relationships to sustain them.
5. Build a stronger network of relationships with suppliers that possess complementary competencies.
6. Increase capital investment on highly flexible, automated machines capable of producing lower volumes of products in greater variety.

CHAPTER SEVEN

Driving down purchase costs

Overview

1. Responding to competitive trading environments
2. Avoiding the top line–bottom line trade–offs
3. Price down–cost down–cost out initiatives
4. Achieving tactical control
5. Targeting the full purchasing portfolio
6. Impacting total cost of acquisition
7. Target costing and product profitability

The Bottom Line

The purchased content of goods and services continues to climb. In many sectors, it is well over 60% of total business costs. Minor, incremental change in cost reduction is inadequate. Senior management should focus on transforming, rather than just managing, the cost base. This calls for a proactive, targeted approach with the injection of radical new business practice across the complete supply chain. Target costing is central to this strategy.

The relentless pressures for cost reduction

'It really comes back to cost. If you really can't change the revenue side much, it comes back to cost.' John Devine, Finance Director, Ford's US Automotive Operations, on their $1 billion annual cost-cutting target.

In many ways the past decade has provided a natural platform for supply chain management and, in particular, innovative strategies of cost reduction. Manufacturing, financial and public service organizations are facing relentless pressure for improvement to bottom line profitability. All of us, as customers, have higher expectations of value for money. As consumers of goods and services, we want convenience, on-time delivery, quality, and high levels of innovation, but all at the lowest possible price.

The result in the manufacturing sector of business is that branded and consumer products companies worldwide are experiencing the growing pressures of what has been termed 'value retailing'. Trading environments are becoming tougher and more competitive. At the same time there is much greater price sensitivity from retail customers and end consumers. Not surprisingly, in such circumstances, the demands for quality and service increase continuously. But there is also an expectation that such enhanced value delivery will be provided at a lower price. Ignore this value–price squeeze and you simply go out of business.

Public sector bodies, agencies and government departments worldwide are also struggling to come to terms with significant changes in organization and business practice. They have all become aware of the accelerating commercial pressures associated with market testing, outsourcing, privatization and similar value-for-money initiatives. Equally, there is much greater cost control pressure from hospitals, schools, utilities and transport bodies.

Such pressures are forcing these private and public sector bodies to look for new areas of strategic direction and operational improvement. This is prompting further reassessment of the role of suppliers and the supply chain as a source of profit improvement and dramatic cost reduction. Such scrutiny will increase; particularly, as was seen in Chapter Two, since the proportion of outsourced business to third party suppliers is also increasing year on year. The cost structures, internal processes and ways of working between purchasers and suppliers are becoming crucial factors contributing to business profitability.

Figure 7.1

Avoid trading off top line growth and bottom line contribution. The trick is to do both, simultaneously, in a planned manner

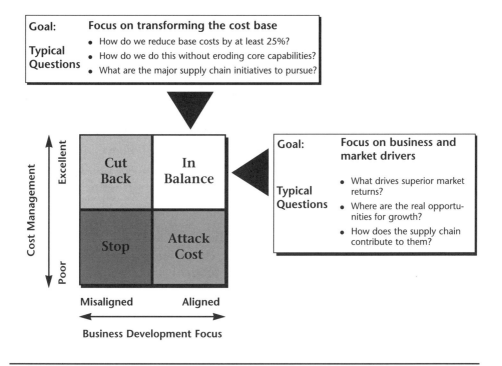

Closing the back door of business

The conclusion must be that, as executive management, internal or external customers, you should be demanding evidence of significant supply chain improvement in costs. It is then for your staff to define and implement the necessary campaigns of planned cost reduction. But, as is argued in Figure 7.1, this should not be seen as a stand alone initiative isolated from the business.

All business sectors now require a focus on cost management. It is the nature, style and radicalism of the approach to the supply chain that differs. While there is no 'one best way', both tactical and strategic initiatives need to be identified.

Some staff, particularly in sales and marketing, may be inclined to block or pay lip service to such cost initiatives. Indeed, it is often argued that the customer facing front of the business is where executive attention should be concentrated. There are few sectors that can now afford such a one-dimensional approach. A client of one of the authors of this book once emphasized that 'it is too easy to leave the back door of business wide open'. This chapter will show you how to close it.

Aggressive attack on the cost base

Over the past fifteen years the major automotive manufacturers, and more recently a number of leading retailers in North America and Europe, have pursued a strategy of lean supply. One element has been a policy of year-on-year cost reduction from their suppliers. As can be seen in Figure 7.2, a wide range of cost change initiatives can be detected. Some of these are very tactical, short-term 'quick hits'.

Figure 7.2

Recognize that a wide range of 'price down–cost down–cost out' initiatives are available. They can be tactical or strategic

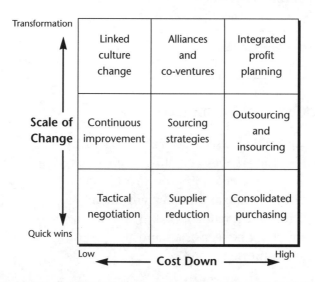

Others will impact total business process inside the company and across the supply chain.

Driven by the highly competitive markets in which they operate, and their inability to increase or even maintain margins by raising prices to their customers, some companies are adopting a top down approach to driving lower prices and increased value from their suppliers. Make no mistake – many of these drives have been impositional, confrontational and one-sided. Power and coercion have been the principal levers of change. The British Steel case is fairly typical.

Case Study:
British Steel
Imposed demands on suppliers to cut their prices

In mid 1997, British Steel announced that they intended to demand sharp and sustained price cuts from their 1,500 suppliers of goods and services. This initiative was in response to exchange rate pressures and declining global competitiveness. It was part of a three-pronged attack on their cost base that also included job cuts and expansion in higher productivity overseas manufacture.

At the time, Sir Brian Moffat, Chairman, declared: 'we have decided that this time, as well as going for efficiency ourselves, we will put the squeeze on the guys who supply us. We are asking them what they are going to do to help us stay competitive and justify being with us in the long term.' The method of persuasion was simple, tactical and coercive. Supplier reduction was to be the lever. 'We will have fewer suppliers in due course, because some will say that if they can have "X" more volume, then they can give a price that is "Y" less.'

The need for profit improvement

There is no reason to believe that these 'cost down' pressures will abate. Indeed, based on experience in other fields of innovative business management, it is expected that this trend will gain momentum and extend across an increasingly large number of business sectors. Without doubt, many sectors will be exposed to a 'double whammy' of inability to increase prices to customers (as a means of offsetting cost increases elsewhere), combined with year-on-year price increases from suppliers. Urgent action is then needed to deal with the squeeze on margins and pressure on profits. Clearly, the approach, methods and change management techniques employed may well differ markedly on a sectoral basis. This is a theme that will be explored in much greater detail in the next chapter.

Capture the opportunities: share the benefits

Effective and sustainable cost reduction is not just about applying pressure on suppliers. That is only a tactical, short-term solution to an immediate problem that a company faces. In some circumstances it can be a complete failure, particularly if the purchaser has little power or leverage over the supply base. We believe that the only successful way forward is to transform purchasing activity fundamentally from its often narrow, functional focus into a more strategic and business-driven process. The key concepts and guiding principles of such an approach are that:

- there is a limit to the amount of internal cost reduction that any company can undertake – the law of diminishing returns takes effect quite quickly;
- external, bought-in purchases of goods and services now represent 60% plus of many businesses' total sales revenue;
- substantial areas of this expenditure have received little professional attention in terms of commercial best practice, value improvement and target cost reduction;
- leveraged, impositional, coercive purchasing is limited in what it can achieve in the medium to long term;
- suppliers are often experts in their areas of specialism and their expertise should be tapped to locate and deliver both cost reduction and value enhancement;
- suppliers should be fully supporting manufacturing and product development, particularly through early involvement at the design stage;

- suppliers are trading partners, not the enemies of purchasing;
- the purchaser–supplier interface, and its active management, is vital for the survival of many companies;
- there is a need for a fundamental change in the way suppliers and purchase costs are managed;
- equally, purchasers need to become much more receptive to feedback and management from their suppliers;
- mechanisms have to be devised to share the benefits of cost reduction between the participants in a manner that is equitable and motivational.

Applying these principles, and making change happen, may require fundamental reorganization of a business; realignment of previously held responsibility, authority and accountability; the resources necessary to manage it; sufficient training to make it work; and prolonged senior management support and involvement. The CRINE Initiative demonstrates how you have to be prepared for the long haul.

'I'm not embarrassed to say: 'Put pressure on them'. I'm not timid about that. All these small companies that serve us, the machine shops around all of our plants, are gone if we lose the competitive business. If we go out of the turbine business in Schenectady, it's lights out for all the entrepreneurs that have done so wonderfully serving us.' John F. Welch Jr., Chairman, General Electric Co.

Case Study:
The CRINE Initiative
Cut costs. Change working practice. Banish bureaucracy.

CRINE is the Cost Reduction Initiative for the New Era. It began in 1992 across oil and gas operations on the UK continental shelf. While progress has been slow, the goal is huge – a 30% plus reduction in capital and a 50% reduction in operational costs of future developments.

Backers include global operators Chevron, Elf-Enterprise and Phillips Petroleum; contractors AMEC, Brown & Root and Foster Wheeler; and suppliers such as Industrial Control Services

and Masoneilan.

CRINE is a catalyst for the industry. The aim is to transform cost structures by transforming working practice. This covers dramatic simplification of the bidding procedures and pre-qualification processes; trimming vastly over-elaborate specifications and producing generic standard terms and model contracts.

It's a simple message. You cannot align purchaser–supplier objectives when you're bogged down in bureaucratic bidding.

Transformational change in costs, rather than incremental improvement, will only come about in those businesses committed to the processes recommended within this chapter and prepared to inject the resource and expertise necessary to make them effective. This cannot be stressed too much. Failure to evaluate and then apply the required resources will quickly render the approach ineffective at best, while at worst it could severely impact supplier relationships and actually increase purchased costs.

You need to build a clear picture of the driving forces, thinking and actions which have led to the current purchasing pattern for any specific category of expenditure. Having fully understood the rationale behind sourcing, you are then in a position to challenge it.

Tactical control through purchasing category management

Initially, many organizations are uncertain how best to move forward when launching a purchasing cost improvement programme. Clearly, as was emphasized above, this begins with senior management commitment. Bringing about permanent change in cost structures will involve introducing new practices, challenging established procedures and creating more demanding expectations of what has to be achieved. This calls for 'champions of change' to sponsor the programme. It also calls for data.

A first step is to assess systematically the current focus on the full purchasing portfolio. Identify the complete range of production and non-production categories of expenditure that comprise total spend. Figure 7.3 is a typical example to illustrate this, drawn from the pharmaceuticals sector. Now address the following questions, in a searching manner, with regard to each of these categories.

- What recent analysis has been made of the expenditure on the category?
- Why is the product, item or service that comprises the category purchased?
- What purchasing methods, tools and techniques are being applied?
- How does the expenditure on the category break down in terms of individual business sites and across specific suppliers?
- Who are the 'influencers of sourcing', i.e. functional

staff who are directly or indirectly involved with suppliers?

- What criteria have been applied in supplier selection and within what type of decision-making process?
- How has sourcing been managed over the past one to five years?
- What price trend data are available, and have cost drivers behind these prices been analysed?

Without data, you cannot move forward. Be prepared to find an absence of analysis in substantial areas of spend. These are the prime opportunities.

Figure 7.3

Identify the purchasing portfolio. Ensure that you cover total spend. Then prioritize the cost reduction targets for attack

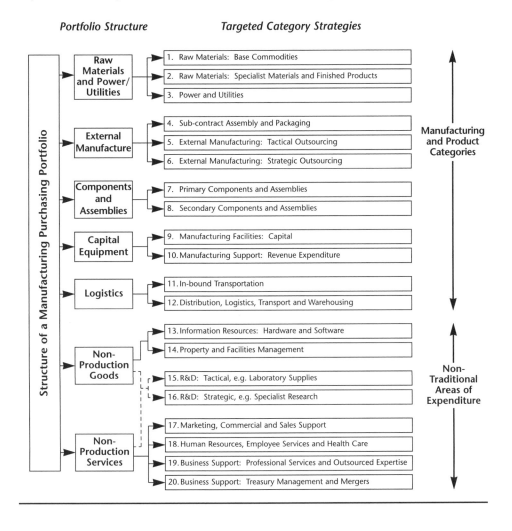

- How long have current suppliers been used?
- What is their performance, and how has that been measured?
- What in-company preferences, local ties, links and dependencies are there with specific suppliers?
- To what extent are these helping or hindering the attainment of required business deliverables?
- What is the current status and nature of the relationship with each supplier?
- In what way should these relationships change?
- What is the record of suppliers in delivering innovation, facilitating technology transfer and supporting quality initiatives?
- What is the quality of management within prime suppliers?
- What is their likely response to cost down initiatives?
- What potential sources of risk and vulnerability exist with core suppliers?
- What plans are in place to reduce or remove them?
- What methods of contracting and payment are being employed?
- How effectively are these meeting the needs of both parties?
- When are contracts to be renegotiated?
- What is the preferred forward sourcing plan over a period of not less than three years?

Challenging past thinking in this way is at the heart of purchasing category management. This is illustrated by the SmithKline Beecham case study. Cross-functional teams should be tasked with reviewing each of the major areas of expenditure and producing forward sourcing plans. This process requires the generation of options, their systematic evaluation, and then the determination of an appropriate implementation plan. The key is a readiness to challenge the status quo and for the business to be open to creative alternatives. Senior management should demonstrate their determination to seek out new and radically different ways of moving forward. Pursuing such a route invariably leads to major breakthrough change.

Integrate source planning within the company's strategy process. Give it the same status as brand planning and capital investment appraisal.

Case Study:

SmithKline Beecham

Realigning costs in more competitive markets through category management

Pharmaceutical businesses are increasingly focused on managing their supply chains more effectively. Downward price pressure from governments and health maintenance organizations in the early 1990s acted as the spur for change. The goal is now to become low cost producers.

SmithKline Beecham (SB) is the benchmark standard in supply chain practice. A series of global initiatives are under way, designed to strengthen core capabilities, improve operating efficiencies and deliver superior value to customers. The deliverables are profitability, longer term business competitiveness and preferred customer status across the worldwide supplier network.

At the heart of SB's purchasing programme is category management. Eight strategies are being pursued.

1. Attain managed control of all high value added purchased categories of expenditure. Attack this £4 billion spend via six broad category families: raw materials; packaging components; external manufacturing; capital equipment; non-production goods; non-production services.

2. Standardize purchasing processes across countries. Significantly ratio-nalize the supplier base.

3. Manage categories at the most appropriate geographical level. Adopt a migration plan: site to country, country to region, and region to global.

4. Create a highly competent purchasing resource. Ensure that sourcing strategies reflect defined linkage to business needs.

5. Accelerate significant improvement in cross-sector and cross-functional co-ordination.

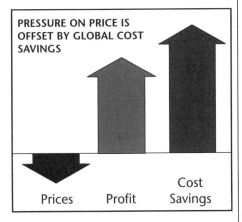

PRESSURE ON PRICE IS OFFSET BY GLOBAL COST SAVINGS

Prices   Profit   Cost Savings

6. Realign resources from transactional to higher value added activity.

7. Drive out complexity through business and supplier integration.

8. Prepare the supply base for future strategic business and manufacturing initiatives.

Impacting total cost of acquisition

The task for both the purchasing organization and the supplier is to enhance the value delivered by increasing the functionality of the product or service while reducing the total cost. This draws on value analysis and value engineering techniques to identify, and then eliminate or minimize, all non-value adding processes and activities in the supply chain. The emphasis, therefore, is on the total acquisition cost of supply and the value it brings to the end product. This requires the support and commitment of all functional disciplines within both the buyer's business and the supplier's business. Using this approach, the aim is to:

- **delete**: eliminate non-value adding activities;
- **reduce**: minimize or eliminate usage;
- **downgrade**: ensure appropriate quality that is 'fit for function';
- **substitute**: identify and introduce alternative products or processes;
- **replace**: use something else;
- **standardize**: minimize or eliminate complexity;
- **integrate**: mesh in the processes and activities of production between the purchaser and supplier.

Structuring an effective cost management programme

When introducing planned purchase cost management, four sequential stages can usually be detected. They are illustrated graphically in Figure 7.4. Initially, there is 'price drift'. This occurs when senior management have little real focus or grip on the supply chain. There are few cost controls. Price is determined by the market place. Inflationary price increases from suppliers are common, and tactical skirmishing is the norm. Not surprisingly, relationships are invariably adversarial.

'Price down' marks the beginning of a true cost management campaign. It is about introducing straightforward tools to identify supplier strengths and weaknesses. In addition, tactical interventions such as supplier reduction, negotiation and cost analysis will achieve some reduction in supplier pricing.

'Cost down' and 'cost out' drives are radically different. They signal a business shift to more strategic cost management and the introduction of increasingly sophisticated margins analysis, capability development, supplier integration and profit planning processes. The goal is to achieve fully transparent and jointly controlled purchaser–supplier development programmes capable of

'Today, quality is not a barrier at all, but we have to come down the cost curve.' Paul Allaire, Chairman & CEO, Xerox.

Figure 7.4

Executives need to lead business initiatives that address both tactical and strategic cost management through phased change

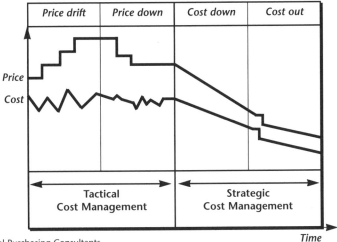

© ADR International Purchasing Consultants.

taking cost out of the supply chain. Integrated within this approach is a similar drive to maximize value from suppliers.

Determining appropriate category strategies

Within the source planning process referred to earlier in this chapter, it is important that team members consider the full range of potential options for cost reduction using the price down–cost down–cost out model. Furthermore, this will

'Cutting costs without improvements in quality is futile.' W. Edwards Deming.

need to reflect the inherent complexity and centrality of the various categories of expenditure to any company's customer and product objectives. This is shown in Figure 7.5 below.

Figure 7.5

Different categories of expenditure demand different approaches to drive down cost. Resources need to be allocated accordingly

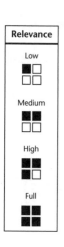

Relevance

Low

Medium

High

Full

Category Examples	Price Down		Cost Down		Cost Out	
	Negotiation	Rationalization	Value Engineering	Joint Development	Target Costing	Profit Planning
Stationery						
Castings						
Packaging						
Computers						
Capital						
Consultancy						
Advertising						
Own Label Goods						
Key Components						
Total Product						

Consider the following sequence:

- segment expenditure by supplier to determine those supply sources which can be controlled through open market competitive forces;
- rationalize the current supply base through a comparative analysis of performance;
- introduce a robust supplier performance assessment process to identify supplier strengths and weaknesses;
- squeeze supplier margins to focus them on cost and value requirements by using market testing, bids, resourcing and negotiation;
- build a thorough understanding of the cost drivers

within the supply chains of likely targets for cost down;

- develop a briefing pack for suppliers, identifying the required way forward (for you and for them);
- visit suppliers to brief them and secure their commitment to the process;
- develop and provide training in value analysis, target costing and profit planning techniques.

Adopting a target cost approach

Many companies worldwide are now adopting a more comprehensive strategic approach to purchase cost management. But we have not yet outlined one of the most effective means by which this is achieved. A paradigm shift occurs when companies extend their thinking beyond mere price and cost reduction into direct delivery of product profitability. Target costing is the process that delivers this goal.

Without extraordinary levels of senior management attention, scrutiny and challenge, do not be surprised if only incremental change is achieved. Transformation in costs is attainable in all supply chains. But final deliverables correlate closely with the quality of executive sponsorship and your active involvement in the defined processes of change.

Typically, however, there is a lot of confusion in the use of the term 'target cost'. It is often applied by design engineers to describe a value analysis or value engineering approach to new product development. An arbitrary cost reduction figure is set, which they then try to achieve. Or it becomes a short-term tactical ploy used by buyers in the negotiation process with suppliers.

Effective target costing is neither of these. It is a methodology which leads to the alignment of final customer perception of product value and functionality, with the design, manufacture, logistics and cost requirements of the business. Not surprisingly, this cannot be achieved without a fundamental redefinition of functional or departmental perspectives. Indeed, target costing goes well beyond purely internally focused process change. It is a transformational step; a strategy driven by the needs of the end customer, with the business aligning its internal processes and external supplier inputs to meet those needs.

Target costing is central to the proposition of 'value delivery', whereby customers select a product because they believe it possesses a superior value (defined as 'benefits

What is your maximum allowable cost for any product or service? Determine your required profit margin. Then calculate this figure. Now put in place the business processes to achieve it.

minus price'). In the sectors where this is the case, business success is dependent on delivering superior value to enough customers at a low enough cost to generate levels of profit that meet or exceed shareholder expectations. Target costing requires the integration of all the functions in a business to deliver customer value profitably.

Business profitability as the process driver

In a true target costing regime, as described in Figure 7.6 and in the case study on Bally, the principal internal driver of the process will be the marketing function or business development group. Their role is to determine the detailed specification of the product strategy. Other input comes from R&D/technical reports on design costs; from manufacturing on volume production start-up and run costs; from purchasing on material costs; and from finance

Figure 7.6

Target costing is a business led strategy driven by customer needs, required profit and shareholder returns. It is usually marketing led

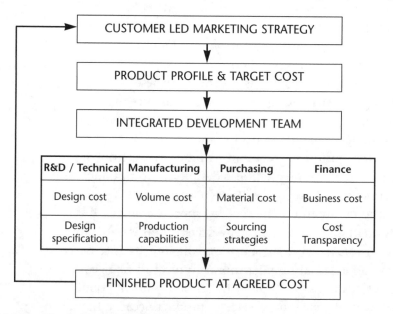

R&D / Technical	Manufacturing	Purchasing	Finance
Design cost	Volume cost	Material cost	Business cost
Design specification	Production capabilities	Sourcing strategies	Cost Transparency

on the business capital, overhead and funding costs. This is all geared to achieving a maximum allowable cost. This process not only determines the value delivered to customers at a given price and the internal costs in the product launch phase. It also prompts a much more searching scrutiny of all the cost and profit requirements at each stage of the product life cycle.

Case Study:

Bally Shoes

Realigning sourcing in more competitive markets through target costing

Bally is one of the world's most exclusive speciality retailers. Its business proposition is dependent on fast response to fashion change, superb quality, and excellent relationships with distributors. This calls for highly flexible, low volume manufacture and creative supply.

Of course, there is a need for appropriate profit contribution that meets shareholder expectations. This drives a premium priced product strategy.

Securing high quality at the lowest cost is at the heart of this product strategy. This called for target costing. Market price minus profit margin equals their target cost.

Internal target costs of design, manufacture, sales and distribution are pre-set. So are the external target costs for leather, soles, accessories and packaging. This becomes the focus for all sourcing strategies.

Achieving supplier target prices now provides a business process for managing Bally profitably.

The objective of target costing, and the team sourcing process that enables it to happen, is to ensure that the appropriate product value is delivered to the customer; the required volumes are maintained; and that the margin contribution is not eroded. The team determines the product price and value required to meet the needs of the customers. Then they calculate the maximum total product cost. Finally, by deduction, they arrive at the profitability of the product. If this does not meet the business and shareholder expectations, then the process continues in an iterative manner.

Target costing drives the attainment of step change in the cost base. It is a powerful tool across the supply chain.

'It will go on. Cutting costs is the hardest thing any executive has to do. But you have no choice about whether you do it. You can only choose when.' Harvey Golub, CEO, American Express.

Driving down purchase costs action checklist

Activities to launch straight away

1. Gather the data on your company's total expenditure with third party suppliers.
2. Form a project team from each of your main business functions. Challenge them to identify the initial cost reduction opportunities for a 'price down' campaign.
3. Sponsor the first wave of 'price down' change. Require teams to deliver quantifiable and readily measurable cost savings within a six to nine month period.
4. Baseline the outputs from the project team with best practice indicators from leading companies, particularly those in low margin and highly competitive sectors.
5. Identify the targets for the next phase of the programme.

Initiatives to make a significant difference

1. Review the progress and learning from the first wave of change. Assess the quality of team leadership and the competence and commitment of team members. Recognize the likelihood of team changes.
2. Highlight the need for a transitional shift from tactical to more strategic cost management. Plan the resource required and set the stretch goals.
3. Mandate and sponsor the launch of a 'cost down–cost out' programme. Ensure that team sourcing actively involves your leading suppliers and trading partners.
4. Introduce more sophisticated business processes and profit planning tools such as target costing. Develop fully open relationships with suppliers and a principled approach to sharing the benefits.
5. Identify non-competing companies, with similar progressive views, in your supply chain. Persuade them to join you in a joint 'cost out' exercise.

CHAPTER EIGHT

Bringing about change

Overview

1. Breakthrough change vs. operational improvement
2. Restructuring roles and responsibilities
3. The power of management by process
4. Options in change management
5. Bottom-up functional change
6. Radical change and radical interventions

The Bottom Line

There is no 'one right way' of bringing about change. The real challenge, therefore, is to define the nature, style and extent of required supply chain initiatives within the context of the demands for change and the levels of internal business support. Such initiatives do not fail due to inherent flaws in concept, vision or strategic intent, but invariably because of inadequacies and shortcomings in implementation. The skills of change management are becoming critical capabilities within the supply chain.

Breakthrough change vs. operational improvement

Ask almost any organization in the public or private sector to identify the issues which are at the top of their priority action list for the next five years and the chances are they will declare that amongst the highest are significant changes in corporate culture, organizational structure, strategic processes and new ways of working. These requirements are invariably described under banners such as 'transformation', 'strategic alignment', 'business process re-engineering' and 'supply chain integration'. Figure 8.1 helps to categorize examples of these programmes by

Figure 8.1

Vast scope exists for improvement across the supply chain. Planned programmes of change will capture the opportunities

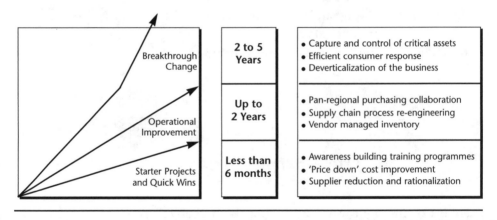

Breakthrough Change	**2 to 5 Years**	• Capture and control of critical assets • Efficient consumer response • Deverticalization of the business
Operational Improvement	**Up to 2 Years**	• Pan-regional purchasing collaboration • Supply chain process re-engineering • Vendor managed inventory
Starter Projects and Quick Wins	**Less than 6 months**	• Awareness building training programmes • 'Price down' cost improvement • Supplier reduction and rationalization

segmenting them into different types based on the likely duration of the required changes and their impact.

Unfortunately, it often seems that companies are being bombarded with what can easily appear to be mere fads and fashions. Indeed, there has never been such a sheer volume of new approaches. This can easily lead executives and operational practitioners, who are famed for their wariness and scepticism of many business 'innovations', to reach one of three incorrect conclusions: firstly, that these new approaches are all hype with no substance and can be dismissed as such; secondly, that they can be ignored as being impractical, conceptual and overly theoretical; or thirdly, that they will not impact the previously neglected area of supply chain management.

Nothing could be further from the truth.   Many perspectives on the supply chain are changing rapidly as top management increasingly focus on to this area as a source of relatively untapped business development opportunity. Figure 8.2 demonstrates this need, and the scope for improvement from such a focus.

Now many readers will be either in charge of change management programmes or likely to be drawn into the issues associated with designing, managing, supporting or participating in them. So it is important to highlight a

'Change is not something that happens. It's a way of life. It's not a process, it's a value. It's not something you do, it engulfs you.' Ronald E. Compton, CEO, Aetna Life.

Figure 8.2

Alignment between business needs and organizational structure in turn drives an internal and external change focus

Organizational Level	Business Focus	Internal Change	External Supply Focus
CEO and The Board	Revenue growth Shareholder value Strategic direction	Business restructuring Product portfolio Strategic capabilities	Supply chain positioning Control of strategic capabilities Alliances and joint ventures
Heads of Business	Business performance Overhead reduction Product roll-out	Quality of staff Cross-unit synergies War on waste	Insourcing vs. outsourcing Board to board involvement Cross-sectoral collaboration
Top Functional Leaders	Functional delivery Superior performance Team motivation	Baselining and bench-marking Functional competence Enablers and processes	Identifying the leaders Supplier capabilities Meshing in processes
Support Staffs	Complexity reduction Competence development Value added activity	Process simplification Improvement programmes Reallocation of resource	Supplier rationalization Joint training plans Value delivery initiatives

number of the key themes central to this area, and then to illustrate them with proven maps through the change management minefield.

Restructuring roles and responsibilities

'Corporations talk about reshaping themselves. But mostly it's just talk.' Rosabeth Moss Kanter on the in-bred resistance to change in large corporations.

Many organizations, and their senior managers involved in change, tend to follow a misguided implicit theory of the ways of trying to bring it about. For example, there is often a misplaced faith in the power of training; maybe 'sheep dip' courses where everyone is 'exposed' to the latest tools and techniques of cost management. Or they attempt to change behaviour by communication programmes, briefing sessions and other similar knowledge sharing activities. While these may be useful exercises in building awareness of the need for business improvement, they do not drive change.

The most powerful ways of changing behaviour, which is at the heart of any change programme, are linked with placing staff into new roles, responsibilities and relationships within very different organizational and supply chain contexts. Creating such situations develops new mind-sets and encourages different ways of thinking about the supply chain. It exposes key staff not only to new ideas but to different paradigms and behaviours. This can either be done 'top down' through radical business restructuring, or 'bottom up' via functionally led improvement programmes. If it is the latter, as shown in Figure 8.3, it may take a considerable amount of time before there is significant business impact.

The power of management by process

In all but the smallest organizations, operational processes have often been carried out, somewhat laboriously, across a range of fragmented 'functions' or departments such as production, design, engineering, marketing, accounts or purchasing. Each would have its own hierarchy, up and down which communication would pass before being transferred down the line to the next department.

Throughout the 1980s, many organizations worldwide came to similar conclusions about the inefficiencies and rigidities associated with the structural weaknesses of this way of working. They began to experiment with means of bridging such vertical structures, either through matrix type arrangements or via semi-permanent project teams, task forces and cross-functional work groups.

Figure 8.3

'Bottom up' change management uses tangible early success to build momentum for broader business-wide transformation

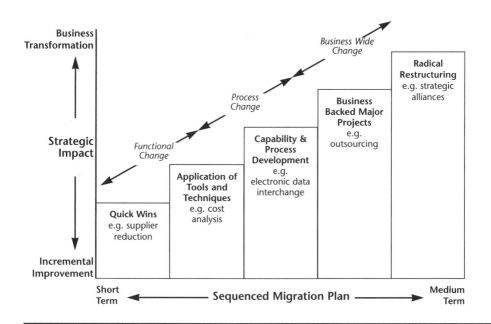

This approach has accelerated over the past decade, and particularly from the early 1990s, as thousands of organizations worldwide were launched on to the business process re-engineering path by Hammer and Champy's influential book, 'Re-engineering the Corporation'. As a management concept, re-engineering, often known by the equally awkward term 'core process redesign', applies a straightforward principle, 'a fundamental rethinking and

'It is rare for any organization to generate sufficient pressure internally to produce significant change in direction. Indeed, internal pressure is likely to be regarded as a form of dissatisfaction with the organization's leadership.' Bruce Henderson, CEO, Boston Consulting Group.

radical redesign of business processes to achieve dramatic improvements in critical measures of performance such as cost, quality, service and speed'. Not surprisingly, it is easy to see the relevance of these goals to the many processes of the supply chain. The key word in the approach is 'radical'. While readers may be aware that re-engineering has many parallels with the old disciplines of work study and time and motion analysis, unlike them it does not just focus on the simplification and improvement of existing processes. Instead it involves transforming an organization from one based on separate 'functions' or specialist departments to one based on the core processes which span most or all of these functional activities. This might cover operational processes such as product development or inventory management, right through to the overall strategic management of the supply chain and the architecture and boundaries of the business.

Figure 8.4

Identify the appropriate constituencies for participation in process redesign. Executives should then act as the sponsors of change

Examples of Supply Chain Processes		Functional Leadership				Executive Sponsorship		
		Pur.	Manuf.	Mktg.	R&D	VPs	MDs	Execs.
Business Strategies	Alliances and joint ventures	○	○	●	▨	▨	▨	●
	Make–buy	●	●	▨	▨	●	●	▨
	Innovation capture	▨	▨	●	●	▨	▨	●
	Insourcing–outsourcing	▨	▨	▨	▨	●	●	●
Operational Improvement	Supplier rationalization	●	▨	▨	▨	●	○	○
	Category sourcing	●	▨	▨	▨	●	▨	○
	Vendor managed inventory	●	●	○	○	○	●	○
	Electronic data interchange	●	●	▨	○	▨	○	●

● High involvement   ▨ Medium involvement   ○ Low involvement

Clearly, depending on the principal focus of supply chain change, the type of leadership and sponsorship will vary, with functional staff driving operational improvement and senior executives leading programmes associated with business development strategy. The linkage between the scale of process change and the nature of constituency sponsorship is shown in Figure 8.4.

Options in change management

It may seem an obvious point, but different business situations clearly need different types of change management. This is often completely misunderstood; sometimes with disastrous consequences for shareholders and stakeholders in the company. In Figure 8.5, we have mapped out a

Figure 8.5

Options in change management need to be assessed and selected in the context of both internal and external factors

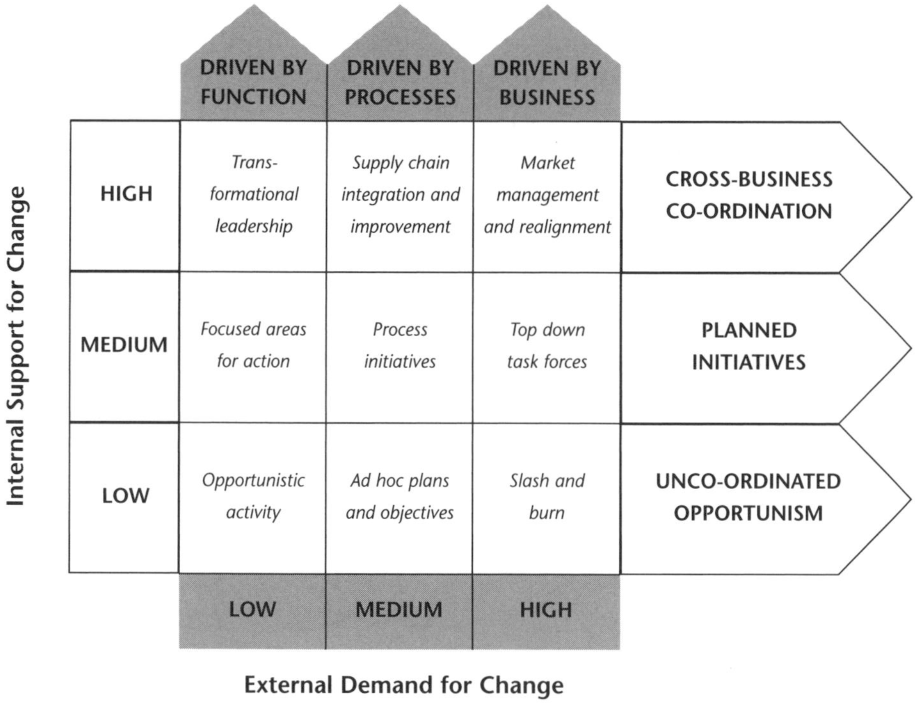

		DRIVEN BY FUNCTION	DRIVEN BY PROCESSES	DRIVEN BY BUSINESS	
Internal Support for Change	HIGH	Trans-formational leadership	Supply chain integration and improvement	Market management and realignment	**CROSS-BUSINESS CO-ORDINATION**
	MEDIUM	Focused areas for action	Process initiatives	Top down task forces	**PLANNED INITIATIVES**
	LOW	Opportunistic activity	Ad hoc plans and objectives	Slash and burn	**UNCO-ORDINATED OPPORTUNISM**
		LOW	MEDIUM	HIGH	

External Demand for Change

powerful way of assessing the different options available within the context of external business circumstances (the demand for change) and the internal environment (the

Be wary of relying only on top-down change. Don't just impose it. Seed it, pilot it, test it. Work hard to raise the level of thinking. Do this up, down and across the business.

level of support for change). Indeed, the drivers for change can be regarded as 'the degree of dissatisfaction with the status quo x the desirability of the vision of the new future x the practicality and necessity of the changes that are proposed'.

Bottom up functional change

A lot of change is driven by functional experts. They may have been appointed to bring about specific supply chain improvements, or they may just be motivated by the desire to implement 'best practice'. This type of change is typical of organizations that are not yet facing radical upheaval or which are operating in relatively stable and profitable markets. The SmithKline Beecham example is typical. It was led by their worldwide heads of purchasing.

Figure 8.6

Bottom up functional change can produce significant business improvement. But it has minimal strategic impact

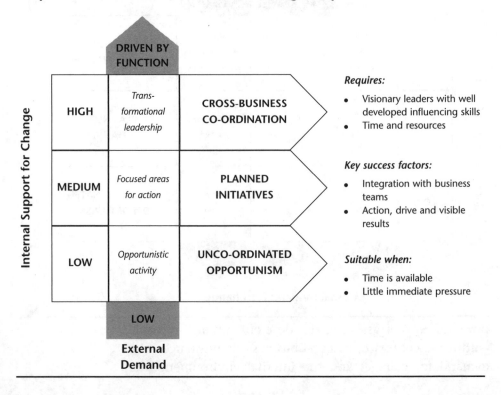

Such programmes tend either to be ad hoc and relatively unco-ordinated, driven by local issues and immediate business problems, or to demonstrate high levels of cross-functional co-ordination. A crucial success factor, though, is the ability of the change leaders to involve a critical mass of staff and build their understanding of the need for change. This invariably revolves around workshops and briefing events. It calls for high levels of presentational and interpersonal competencies.

Select change leaders as much for their interpersonal and facilitative skills as for their technical functional competence.

Case Study:
SmithKline Beecham
Using cascade training and functional change to capture post-merger synergies

When SmithKline French and the Beecham Group PLC merged in 1989, the resulting corporation, SmithKline Beecham (SB) became one of the world's largest healthcare companies. With 50,000 employees selling 300 product lines and laboratory services in 130 countries, SB had sales, at that time, of over £5 billion.

The cost of external purchases was over £3 billion and represented 55% of sales revenue. In 1990, however, purchasing was an undervalued function. There were no formal training and development programmes for staff. Little transfer of best practice was taking place. Staff were inadequately focused. Profit improvement was not yet on the agenda.

To change this, SB launched a three year worldwide programme – Simply Better Purchasing – and targeted savings of £100 million.

A cascade development programme was designed to facilitate the required

clarity of focus and boost functional competence:

1. A one-week launch conference was held for top purchasing directors worldwide.

2. Two phases of one-week long training workshops were run for over 400 members of staff and 50 senior operations executives.

3. At-the-job coaching was facilitated by train-the-trainer workshops for 25 directors of purchasing.

Most importantly, the programme was geared not just for the full-time purchasing community but for all staff with significant influence on sourcing and supplier management decision making. Attendees were drawn from marketing, research and development, clinical trials, technical and information resources departments.

Savings of £75 million in the first 18 months led to a doubling of the target to £200 million. This was achieved with ease.

Process driven change

When the pressures for change are moderate, a wide range of process interventions are appropriate. It is also usually easier to secure staff attention when there is greater awareness of the external competitive pressures. Volvo, for example, is now well aware of the need to drive a number of fundamental supply chain improvements across the business. Major process interventions include:

- simplification and standardization of manufacturing capabilities;
- using joint ventures to access innovative production techniques;
- focusing on suppliers as a prime source of design input and involving them much earlier in the new product development cycle;

Do not regard process redesign as simply about cutting head count. Many core processes can be dramatically improved. The quantum of change is frequently in excess of 25%, and can be considerably higher. Segment your business processes into the core strategic ones as well as those that provide a supportive role. Then change them.

Figure 8.7

Redefinition, restructuring and redesign of core business processes is a credible response to moderate change drivers

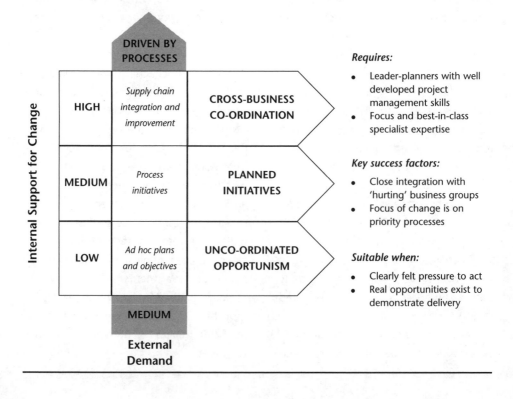

- integrating demand and supply management from suppliers through to end customers and consumers;
- completely reorganizing local, regional and global sourcing responsibilities.

There are also many sub-processes within the supply chain that need to be redesigned, albeit at an operational rather than a more strategic level. These include:

- transactional simplification of requisitioning and order processing;
- closer integration of accounts payable, sales order processing and purchasing systems;
- strengthening of purchaser–supplier interfaces via autofax and electronic data interchange (EDI);
- reorganizing sourcing teams into cross-functional groups;
- sharing and transferring best practice across sites and business sectors or divisions.

'We cannot downsize to reach sustainable favourable profit-ability. Our strategy involves both expansion and tightening.' Leif Johansson, CEO, Volvo, on announcing a three year drive to cut costs, raise productivity and accelerate product development.

Taking such processes and assessing the scope for raising productivity and delivering superior performance is the

---

Case Study:
Volvo
Cutting costs, boosting productivity and rolling out new models

Volvo, the Swedish automotive group, is an under-performing, lacklustre niche player. Operating margins have been as low as 1.8%. An overdue three-year strategic initiative was launched in 1998. The approach is classic process management with an overriding priority to raise productivity. How?

1. Slim down management by one third. Implement a much leaner, simpler decision-making structure.
2. Cut purchasing and sourcing costs by 15% during the three year period.
3. Accelerate product launches.

4. Introduce one new product range every year within each of their six divisions.
5. Cut development costs to lower product break-even points. Design vehicles that share common platforms. Reduce the platforms from three to two.
6. Seek out joint ventures in different product areas. Develop closer and more co-operative relationships with suppliers.

This is all designed to achieve a targeted operating margin of 5-7% and annual revenue increases of 10%.

Radical change needs rapid adaptation. Use shock tactics and executive driven task forces to grab staff attention. Make the required direction of change explicit. Don't allow consultation and team work to delay the necessary initiatives.

essence of redesign of core supply chain processes. It should involve a fundamental rethink and searching challenge of how an organization develops, sources and delivers its products or service to either an internal or an external customer. Not surprisingly the approach has been taken up with a vengeance, particularly within the medium sized and larger corporations and across major public sector bodies in government.

Radical change: radical interventions

Businesses that require radical change are invariably those that have to adapt or die. The more urgent the situation, the more the business requires change drivers. Active, robust leadership is required. The range of options

Figure 8.8

When external demand for change is high, it is crucial that top executives provide visible and resolute leadership

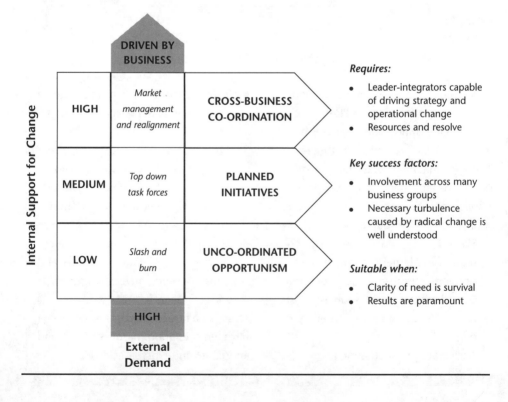

described in Figure 8.8 can be found in many of the 'back from the brink' case studies.

Without doubt, a driving, visionary executive team is capable of reconfiguring business structure in response to crisis situations. There will be a need to alter fundamentally the strategic, competitive and operational capabilities of the organization in such circumstances. This is most definitely the case with Pilkington's.

Expect to cut back or realign internal manufacturing. Consider substantial programmes of outsourcing. Refuse to accept current levels of productivity. Restructure and reposition the company within its value stream. Downsize if needed, but make sure the focus remains on the future.

'I strongly believe that companies don't fail because they can't strategize; it is because they can't execute. Thinking doesn't change a business, essential as it is. Action changes a business.' Dick Brown, CEO, Cable & Wireless.

Case Study:
Pilkington
Executives in glass houses need to throw stones

Pilkington's is a classic example of a former monopolist whose domination in the market place has ended. The company invented the spectacular float glass process, took out the patents and sat back and collected the profits. Trouble only set in when the patents ran out. In 1997, a new CEO was appointed in Paolo Scasoni. His job is to turn around the world's largest manufacturer of glass, and cut out over £200 million of excess cost.

1. The business is to be restructured. 6,000 jobs across the European workforce will go.
2. Loss-making businesses are to be eliminated. Across Europe, 60 of the 174 downstream building products sites will be sold or closed down. These are all at the lower end of the value chain in builders' merchant operations and double glazing units.
3. There will be a big drive on manufacturing and supply chain effectiveness. The productivity gap with rivals such as Saint-Gobain will be closed.

The real challenge, however, is to change the archaic, decentralized, robber-baron culture of separate operating units, autonomous boards, non-collaborating functions. As the CEO describes it, 'Pilkington's is less of a company, more of a technological and financial confederation.' Each of these fiefdoms is to be dismantled. For the first time, collaboration across the supply chain and leveraging of resources and suppliers is possible.

Bringing about change action checklist

Activities to launch straight away

1. Locate sponsors, enthusiasts and supporters of supply chain change at an early stage. Mobilize commitment through cross-functional joint diagnosis of the issues.
2. Use workshops and briefing sessions to raise the level of thinking about available initiatives. Do this at the centre, up, down and across the business.
3. Focus on to 'quick wins' and immediate opportunities. Produce deliverables and outputs rather than abstractions. Make change tangible.
4. Give your initial programme of change some form of identity.
5. Concentrate the initial wave of change on breaking down barriers between departments.

Initiatives to make a significant difference

1. Identify an appropriate and effective change management methodology. This will minimize the risks of complex and radical interventions.
2. Set the supply chain agenda, orchestrate the overall programme and frame demanding stretch goals that are focused on substantial gaps in competitiveness.
3. Do not delegate the implementation of strategic change. Provide the top management direction that is needed in a highly visible manner.
4. Define a limited number of business mission critical supply chain processes. These must be central to the strategic intent of the company. Ensure they have maximum financial impact. Change them.
5. Shake up the power structure inside the business. De-layer management, restructure operations, divest non-core activities. Be prepared to destabilize the status quo.

CHAPTER NINE

The electronic supply chain

Overview

1. Application of enabling technologies
2. Operational improvement vs. strategic positioning
3. Transformational potential of the technologies
4. Connectivity in the supply chain
5. Impact on market structures
6. Commercial application of electronic trading
7. Integrating technology and business relationships
8. From 'push' supply to 'pull' demand chains

The Bottom Line

Business needs to do a lot more than just place orders electronically. The complete supply chain can be impacted by the technologies of electronic commerce, and redesigned accordingly. Transform the way your organization creates markets and delivers products to customers.

Connectivity and the electronic revolution

A fundamental shift in economics and electronic commerce is under way; a shift that is less about actual technology than about new commercial behaviour and different responses towards acquisitions and the supply chain. Millions of people at home, work and university are communicating electronically using readily accessible, open standards. Within this electronic universe, many users have begun purchasing goods, services and materials. After the false dawns of electronic data interchange (EDI) and electronic funds transfer (EFT), this explosion in connectivity is the latest – and for business strategists the most important – wave in the electronic commerce revolution. We believe that it will truly enable the creation of an electronic supply chain.

Figure 9.1

Focus less on the technologies than on the ways in which they impact on competitiveness. Regard them as enablers of change

Electronic Commerce	Conducting or enabling the purchasing, marketing and selling of goods or services through electronic networks.
Electronic Data Interchange	A way of passing structured documents, such as purchase orders, forecast data and invoices, from one company to another.
Efficient Consumer Response	A mechanism to translate pull driven consumer demand into efficient supply through integrated retailer–supplier systems.

Challenging the rules of business

Over the past decade, managers have focused on adapting their operating processes to embrace new technologies that offer additional routes to market. Dramatic as these operating changes have been, a more profound transformation of the business landscape lies ahead. Executives – and not just those in high-tech or traditional retail and trading companies – will be forced to rethink the strategic fundamentals of their businesses. Over the next decade, the economics of electronic commerce, and its impact on where and how customer–supplier relationships are conducted, will precipitate profound change in the structure of entire sectors of the economic landscape and in the ways individual companies compete.

Application around clusters of technologies

In this rapidly emerging area it can be difficult to avoid framing clear definitions without drawing in too much detail on the core technologies and processes explained in Figure 9.1. This is particularly true in view of the breakthrough advances taking place in the required infrastructures and the acceleration in computing, media and internet applications.

'As far as processors are concerned, Moore's Law still holds, and power can be expected to double every year for 15 or more years, taking us to 2010 and beyond. And band width is also doubling every year. This means we are heading for a highly interconnected world.' Eric Schmidt, CEO and Chairman of the Board, Novell.

We would argue that it is not necessarily helpful to understand the concept of the electronic supply chain through the technology alone. It is essentially a preferred way of doing business, a guiding methodology and an integrated set of business practices. When combined they generate improved operating efficiency and substantial opportunities for reducing costs. But as well as stimulating such operational improvements they can trigger a redefinition of the market place and secure potentially new sources of competitive advantage. As has been emphasized in the earlier chapters of this book, such strategic positioning will only accrue to those organizations with the capability and determination to look beyond the short-term gain and properly evaluate the options available for transforming the way markets are created, products and services produced and customers satisfied.

Redefining the supply chain

There are five main ways in which electronic innovation is impacting the supply chain and creating or redefining the market place:

- **dematerialization**: reduction, removal and redeployment of substantial assets invested in traditional sales and marketing;

- **disintermediation**: compression in the length of the supply chain through the elimination of middle men in the sales process. Encyclopedia Britannica is a typical example;
- **deverticalization**: creation of extended enterprises, linked manufacturers and inter-industry groups operating within new electronic markets;

Case Study:
Encyclopedia Britannica
Electronic communication cuts across traditional customer relationships

Fundamental change has been required in the marketing of this internationally known brand. It was a casualty of electronic commerce.

Since 1990, sales of Britannica's multi-volume sets had dropped by more than 50%. CD-Roms have devastated the printed encyclopedia business. The reason is simple.

Encyclopedia Britannica was selling for somewhere in the region of $1,500 to $2,200. An encyclopedia on CD-Rom, such as Microsoft's Encarta, retails for around $50. And many people receive Encarta free since it arrives bundled with their personal computer purchase. The cost of producing a set of encyclopedias – printing, binding and distribution – is between $200 and $300. The cost of producing a CD-Rom is $1.50. Such is the impact of technology shift and the emergence of new competition. It can radically, and terminally, disrupt the conventional value proposition, even of such a well established business. Why was Encyclopedia Britannica so vulnerable?

1. Encarta's content is licensed from the Funk & Wagnalls encyclopedia. This was historically sold in supermarkets. Microsoft merely spruced up the content with public domain illustrations and movie clips. It was too easy for Encyclopedia Britannica to view this as a toy. Parents, however, regarded it as education, meeting the same goal as a 'proper' encyclopedia.

2. Britannica was also highly dependent on the economics of its costly distribution channel – intensive personal selling. This laid it wide open to competitive attack.

Other sectors, such as automobiles, real estate, travel insurance and even long distance telecommunications and containerized freight services, face the same potential challenge from electronic commerce. How well prepared are they?

- **data integration**: real time access, capture and transfer of data between trading partners;
- **development of new products**: which support, sustain and extend electronic commerce.

Clearly, as is shown in Figure 9.2, there is scope for both strategic realignment of suppliers with their customers

Figure 9.2

The electronic supply chain offers both strategic advantage and operational improvement. It relies on clusters of technologies

Top Line Growth ◄──── Business Contribution ────► Bottom Line Profit				
Technology Clusters	Market Creation	Customer Impact	Operational Improvement	Transactional Efficiency
Electronic Commerce	Invent a supply chain	Pull vs. push sales	Global sourcing	Paperless purchasing
Efficient Consumer Response	Comparative advantage	On-time delivery	Inventory reduction	Order management
Electronic Data Interchange	Data warehouse	Data access	Data integration	Data transfer
High ◄──── Transformational Potential ────► Moderate				

and within their value chains as well as huge potential for improvements in day-to-day operational effectiveness. Senior executives are advised to assess the full potential of such realignment.

While it is impossible to predict with any certainty by how much and how quickly supply chain redefinition will take place in all sectors, there are many reasons to believe that consumers and businesses will eventually transact huge volumes of business and sales on-line and, not surprisingly, dramatically increase their dependency on such enabling technologies.

'We are not talking about data or even information – but leveraging the power of knowledge. Most organizations have the knowledge, but it is isolated in islands. We need to build bridges.'
Keith Todd, CEO of ICL.

Figure 9.3

Connectivity across the supply chain provides the opportunity to deverticalize. Other competitive factors determine its aptness

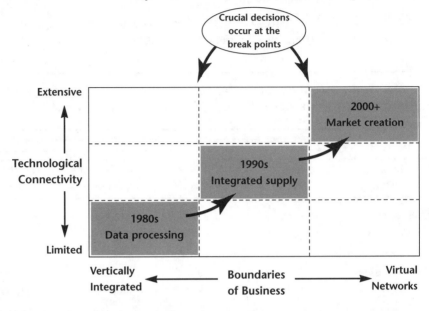

Effect on market structures

'You will see virtual network companies start to evolve, truly global virtual companies. Companies will tie together their own operations in an enterprise network, with those of their customers, suppliers, partners and employees in ways that have never been done before.' John Chambers, President and CEO, Cisco Systems.

Without doubt, the increased potential of technological connectivity, as conceptualized in Figure 9.3, offers entrepreneurs opportunities to break into new markets.

Already we have seen a number of revolutionary changes within established sectors such as retailing, publishing and the information industry. There is also great scope for suppliers in the developing world, such as those associated with the Asian Sources Media Group, to use the internet as a showcase for their wares.

One of the first on-line ventures was the Internet Shopping Network. It started life as a handful of people, a superb virtual brochure, a couple of borrowed Sun servers, no stock and a subsidized distribution deal with a computer industry giant. This was the antithesis of the monolithic, vertically integrated bureaucracy.

Jeff Bezos's amazon.com is often cited as the paradigm of a successful web business and a showcase for inventory free retailing. But even though it has 600,000 customers and 400 employees, and was floated on the New York Stock Exchange for $250 million, it has not yet made any profit! It has also triggered a bitter price war with competitors. The learning to date, though, is that technology alone does not provide business advantage. Amazon goes a long way beyond being a virtual catalogue. It has succeeded over other internet bookstores because it places due emphasis on entertainment and fun. Customer engagement is crucial. You have to tempt the customers to access your business. But it is then the nature of the total offering that converts the enquiry into sale.

Internet trading and web sites reverse the rules of marketing. They involve pull media, not push. You have to draw potential customers into your site and then persuade them to buy.

Case Study:
Asian Sources Media Group
Minnows on the world wide web

Thousands of minute companies across China, Asia, South America and the Indian sub-continent have a huge competitive advantage through labour costs that are often 90% lower than competitors' in the developed world. But global purchasers tend not to be aware of them, since they have few effective distribution channels.

Or at least, they didn't until Internet marketing appeared on the trading scene.

A case example is Asian Sources Media Group (ASM), a publishing company based in Hong Kong. Their web site serves as an entry point into a network of over 7,000 Asian suppliers in Hong Kong, China, Taiwan and Korea. Most of them are very small,

family controlled and highly entrepreneurial manufacturing businesses. With ASM's help and infrastructure, they now receive over 100,000 inquiries a quarter. Negotiation and contracting are conducted electronically by email. Sourcing is facilitated by ASM's on-line catalogue of 200,000 or more products.

Of course, there was a lot of initial wariness and scepticism, which is why ASM employs nearly 500 in-country sales staff who visit factories, train the locals, offer set-up support and generally facilitate the process.

It may be in its infancy, but this type of trading is predicted to grow exponentially. It could revolutionize sourcing of low value items.

'Internet trading is all about reaching markets your existing channels either cannot reach at all, or cannot reach cost effectively.'
Anthony Miller, Research Manager for International Data Corporation, on forecasting that the value of worldwide electronic commerce will increase from $2.6 billion in 1996 to more than $220 billion by 2001.

Easier access to world markets

Electronic commerce has the power to rearrange the geography of markets and supply chains. This involves a lot more effort and strategic consideration than just putting a few web pages on-line! It calls for a thorough audit of the enabling potential of the technology; an in-depth reassessment of the nature of the market within which you operate; an evaluation of the available channels to that market; and, most importantly, real clarity of focus on how you should be positioning your business within it. Clearly, the extent and scope of such a review needs to reflect the size and capital needs of the company under consideration.

Small providers of any sort of consumer goods and non-differentiated services can potentially use the internet to reach customers worldwide at relatively low cost. It gives them visibility and access to markets that they would not be able to consider through the use of previously available sales channels. This encourages the development of new markets and new ways for suppliers and purchasers to find each other in these markets. They can also join forces with other businesses to form trade consortia, either for linked selling or to increase leverage with otherwise inflexible and more powerful suppliers. The UK electricity market case study neatly illustrates this. In addition, there is substantial potential for niche penetration and redefinition of existing approaches to ancillary business processes. This is what Oasis Global Systems have achieved in the car leasing field.

Medium sized businesses usually possess greater information resources, have more sophisticated managerial capabilities and, most importantly, access to considerably greater capital funds. Such SMEs, small and medium enterprises, should be able to integrate electronic commerce readily into their trading strategies. This will extend their reach into new markets. But they can also focus on their complete supply chains and locate the opportunities for more effectively responding to consumer demand and shortening the purchasing cycle.

Large companies should be doing more than just enhancing their individual supply chain processes or focusing solely on cost savings or incremental sales revenue. Since they are in the best position to exploit and leverage the technology, their goal should be either to create new markets or to achieve some form of superior differentiated position within them. Having achieved that, executive attention should then turn to designing better and more efficient processes.

Case Study:
UK Electricity Market
Creating an electronic market place in a deregulated sector

In an attempt to stimulate competition in the UK electricity market place, two major government interventions have occurred over the past decade. Firstly, the regional electricity companies (RECs) have been privatized. Secondly, business and domestic customers can choose which supplier to use.

The 55,000 largest users of electricity can select their suppliers from among the 16 RECs. Some do this by using an electronic market called The Utilities Exchange. This is a computer system including a database that links suppliers with consumers. A user can invite bids, and compare them, electronically.

From 1998, further deregulation will allow another two million businesses to enter the competitive market for electricity supply. Also, purchasing consortia are being formed from those companies not large enough individually to attract a competitive bid from suppliers.

The bottom line? Savings of between 10% and 15% are common when purchasing electricity through the electronic market place.

Dealing with management scepticism

Of course, many executives will remain sceptical about the depth to which electronic commerce is likely to impact their market place and penetrate core business processes.
Consider a fairly typical scenario. A medium sized manufacturer has made some progress on realigning its business practices to accommodate electronic data interchange. This has been marketing led. This same company

Case Study:
Oasis Global Systems
Creating an electronic community using shared technologies

Oasis is a recent winner of the British Telecom Award for Electronic Commerce in small and medium enterprises (SMEs). It is based in Hemel Hempstead, UK.

It has created a trading community for car fleet operators. This makes it cheaper to process repair and maintenance invoices and documents. These currently cost the British fleet industry around £150 million a year in administration.

Each leased car comes with its own smart card. This contains all the details a garage needs to know about maintenance authorization limits. Garages in the community can then send their invoices using EDI to the fleet operators. It is a simple, user friendly scheme for fleet operational improvement.

The electronic supply chain is about knowledge management and process redesign. Information technology is not the solution. That is simply about how pieces of data are transmitted. You need a strategic vision on how to manage this, internally and externally. In other words, regard information as a strategic business capability.

can readily envisage selling its products through a web page. But what level of confidence is felt when they are presented with an opportunity to purchase goods and services from its suppliers through electronic means? This presents an interesting challenge. Should an equivalent business logic be applied to purchasing as was applied to selling? Is there a need to examine more carefully the nature of the linkages between input materials, their complexity and the types of business relationship available with the selected suppliers? Indeed, it is probable that the purchaser–supplier relationships for such transactions, particularly if the goods are highly differentiated, are far too intense to be conducted solely through the medium of electronic commerce. They are certainly very dissimilar to the fleeting spot relationships found in electronic sale transactions for the vast majority of retail or commodity goods and services.

So, in dealing with these concerns, there should be a consideration of the following questions:

■ How should a company control the dissemination and application of commercially valuable information? This is particularly the case when the information is traded between closely linked partners in a strategic business relationship.

- What risks and vulnerabilities may be encountered, and how should they be minimized? It is noticeable that even the most technologically secure organizations have found their computer systems invaded by computer hackers.
- In what ways can electronic technologies support commodity or low value purchasing and supply? There is clearly a straightforward gain in transactional efficiency in this solely price driven arena.
- What differences and complexities will occur in more strategic supply relationships? This is especially relevant in the context of the highly collaborative ventures described in Chapter 4.

'Developments such as the Internet remove some of the inherent advantages that large companies had in their IT networks. Large companies can use e-commerce to do more, but smaller companies can use it to be more.' Alex Drobik, Chairman of the European Electronic Messaging Association.

Commercial application of electronic trading

It is important to form a considered view of how best to utilize electronic commerce across the supply chain.

Unfortunately, the fundamental mistake that many executives may make is to assume that by simply using electronic commerce, 'all troubles' will vanish. Or, moreover, that their business will somehow automatically find itself positioned in an appropriate revenue stream.

The selection of the most effective channel of distribution is clearly a core element of marketing strategy. Whether or not that should include electronic commerce, and its centrality, will be dictated by the specific circumstances of any particular organization and the market it operates in. Rigorous segmentation needs to be applied.

- Which relationship strategies, with suppliers and customers, will secure the maximum value?
- How can electronic commerce support this range of strategies?

Encyclopedia Britannica's problems were more than a parable about the dangers of complacency. They demonstrate how quickly and dramatically the new economics of commerce can change the rules of competition. It allows, under certain conditions, new players and substitute products to render obsolete the traditional levers of competitive advantage such as brand value, content differentiation and sales force effectiveness. Clearly, failure to evaluate the potential emergence of new channels, and their cost and value impact, can have alarming consequences.

Maintaining a relational advantage

Of course, the above argument assumes that the commercial transactions are taking place in leveraged or potentially commodity markets. This is where value is regarded as almost entirely synonymous with price. Encouragingly, this is not an assumption that applies in many areas of business.

Scrutinize the current flows, blockages and delays in the passage of data across the supply chain. Then assess how, by extending and connecting applications beyond an individual enterprise, communication between all the trading players will be improved. Then assess the pay-off.

A company's ability to deliver value consists of all the activities it performs to design, produce, market, deliver and support its product. The value added activities that comprise the total supply chain collectively comprise the sector's total value proposition and its specific configuration of competitors, suppliers, distribution channels and customers. In markets where price and value are not synonymous, executive leaders should ensure competitive advantage is secured by striving to achieve a more favourable supplier–customer configuration (and attendant methods of communication) than their competitors. Electronic commerce in such circumstances plays a very different role from the simple notion of a 'cyberspace bazaar' in which to hawk your wares. It becomes an essential part of the processes being employed to bind value adding relationships together. It can clearly be a medium for enhancing such value.

Its essence is that it can redefine how you design new products and services and the ways in which you involve third parties. This process clearly has both strategic significance as well as scope for operational improvement.

Integrating technology and preferential relationships

Electronic technologies can be integrated within planned strategies of preferential relationship development to add and control value between suppliers and purchasers. So, for example, two companies may have established certain channels of communication built around open behaviour, mutual understanding and shared standards. This, in turn, can be facilitated by links such as electronic data interchange.

It can promote operational advantage from features such as synchronized production systems or shared distribution facilities. Although at the moment this is seriously inhibited by the lack of fully integrated, open access computer networks. This is why the major software companies, such as Microsoft, are so aware of the commercial potential from developing and controlling such a technological asset.

Examples of such value adding relationships include:

- American Airlines, which used access and control of the SABRE reservation system with travel agents to achieve higher levels of capacity utilization than its competitors;
- Wal Mart, which has exploited its EDI links with

'The Internet makes big changes in the way we do business. Only about two per cent of organizations have EDI, but 99 per cent have a PC and a telephone. The Internet creates a critical mass of people who can exchange data over the network.' Matthew Wall, Business Unit Director, EDS.

Case Study:
Microsoft
Developing processes to link the entire value chains of trading companies

The Value Chain Initiative (VCI), led by Microsoft, was launched in September 1996. It is a consortium of 130 independent and alliance linked global businesses, software suppliers, logistics specialists, transportation companies and hardware manufacturers. It also includes the Logistics Institute at Georgia Institute of Technology,

leading universities worldwide and a number of management consultancies.

Its goal is to create an end-to-end, and seamless, business-to-business electronic commerce framework. This will allow companies to integrate value chain applications, regardless of size or format, through 'dynamic information' in real time.

Case Study:

Tesco

Developing an electronic trading community in retail

Tesco is the most successful food retailer in the UK. Developing an electronic trading community of over 1,500 suppliers, across 90% of their sales order volume, using electronic data interchange (EDI), has been an important enabler of their progress to the position of top performer.

Rapid collection and transfer of commercial data has supported quick response to customer needs and an increase in the number of products on sale. Accurate forecasting, just-in-time delivery and a dramatic reduction in stockholding have boosted overall profitability. Top line has been impacted by converting storage space to sales area; bottom line by taking stock out of the supply chain.

In 1982, 80% of dry grocery was distributed direct to individual stores by individual suppliers. Orders were placed manually via supplier representatives. Over the past fifteen years, this supply chain has been transformed. 90% of goods are now delivered to stores from Tesco warehouses. Stock and sales data are routed electronically from stores to head office. Orders are batched up at warehouse level and then sent to suppliers.

Secondly, the internal supply chain was revolutionized by a multi-million pound investment in electronic point of sale technology. This provided the linkage between sales, ordering and the delivery cycle, and gave vital information on product profitability and stock movement.

Finally, EDI drove close integration in the external supply chain by bringing suppliers and Tesco closer together. This process began after electronic invoicing was legalized in the UK in the early 1980s, and accelerated rapidly throughout the 1990s. The process was facilitated by agreed standard software, streamlined testing procedures, extensive communication and training across the European supplier network.

Information management has been the prime enabler of change. The fast, accurate collection of product and customer data has encouraged Tesco to expand dramatically the number of products they offer for sale. Equally, they are able to respond immediately to changes in customer demand.

Achieving success in this area calls for a dual attack. The internal supply chain and the boundaries between functions need to be re-engineered. This, in turn, provides a platform for improving the external supply chain. By taking the initiative for integration in this way, a major company can drive change across a sector.

suppliers to increase its inventory turns dramatically. Indeed, as was seen earlier, the whole concept of efficient consumer response (ECR) is predicated on this style of relationship;

■ Tesco and its development of an electronic retail trading community in the UK.

All three of these businesses compete as much through their skillful manipulation and management of commercial data as they do on the provision of a physical product or service. They have effectively relaxed some of the constraints imposed by the conventional model of value flow being tied inextricably to the linear physical activities of production, supply and distribution. When linked players in strong relationships are connected electronically, value can travel by itself. New ways of adding and appropriating value can then be exploited.

'Collaboratively maintained information systems will be essential to Quick Response relationships going forward. Ten years ago, the issue was whether retailers should share point of sale data with suppliers. That's not the issue now.' David Cole, Chairman & CEO, Kurt Salmon Associates.

Going beyond traditional data exchange

Efficient consumer response (ECR) is about re-engineering the relationships across a complete supply chain to achieve a more appropriate focus on customer or end consumer requirements. It involves all of the companies in that supply chain, or at least the major players, working together to fulfil consumer expectations – better, faster, more responsively and at lower cost. The approach has received intense scrutiny in the retail sector but it is applicable to all sectors with a considerable product or service pipeline and where there is inherent variability in demand.

Electronic trading, usually incorporating electronic data interchange (EDI), is central to the approach in order to remove any reliance on paperwork systems. EDI, of course, has been around a long time. It was first used in the 1960s by the transportation industry to help solve delivery delays that resulted in mountains of paper documents. Over the past thirty years its use has increased; so much so that some major organizations, particularly retailers, require their trading partners to use EDI as a condition of doing business with them.

However, EDI applied independently of other processes merely replaces paper documents such as quotations, purchase orders and invoices with electronic documents transmitted through data networks. On its own it will deliver a number of valuable operational benefits. In particular it brings traditional cost savings in less paperwork, lower mailing costs, improved speed of processing and a reduction in errors. It can also lead to reduced inventory and enhanced cash management.

Case Study:

GE Lighting

Automating non-value added work in MRO purchasing

In many companies, purchasing staff spend far too much time on transactional routines. Valuable resource gets drawn into processing huge volumes of low value MRO-type orders. Serving the factory and shuffling the paper becomes more important than managing the supply chain.

GE Lighting in the USA have cut through this time-wasting using TPN Post internet communication links to suppliers.

Plants generate the requisitions; they are batched up centrally; drawings, specifications, commercial data and sourcing criteria are assembled; requests for quotations (RFQs) are then shipped electronically to current and potential suppliers; responses come back within days, if not hours; on-line assessment is made via qualification screens; there is an immediate award of the contract; the

purchase order is transmitted by electronic data interchange (EDI); and payment is dealt with by electronic funds transfer.

Purchasing staff monitor the process carefully via weekly reports and supplier performance data is accessed via the GE supplier scorecard.

Not surprisingly, suppliers are enthusiastic, since the system helps them gain business. GE purchasers are on board, since they can leverage qualified suppliers into other US locations and worldwide through Europe and Asia Pacific.

The deliverables have been impressive: cost savings of up to 20%; enhanced quality; access to a wider supply network; paperless purchasing; and sourcing time down from two weeks to two days. Most importantly, staff time has been freed up for redirection into high added value supply work.

Clearly, such improvements, and the initiatives to secure them, should not be neglected by senior management nor functional staff. As can be seen in the GE Lighting case study, cost savings and more effective commercial practices can readily be delivered through the application of good practice in process redesign.

Achieving a pull based demand chain calls for high levels of internal and external collaboration. Managing variability, and integrating the supply chain, is as much to do with structured change management as it is with technology.

Moving towards a 'pull' demand chain

The real benefits of the technology, however, are delivered when there is a shift from traditional EDI to a supply chain that integrates sourcing, production, distribution, transportation and stock replenishment in a simultaneous manner.

Figure 9.4

Convert the supply chain from push to pull. Respond to customer driven demand. Use technology to link the chain

Manufacturer led 'push' supply chain. High demand variability. Huge buffer stocks. Little integration.

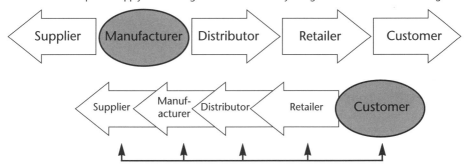

Customer led 'pull' demand chain. Rapid data exchange. Low stocks. Quick response. High integration.

Traditionally, as is shown in Figure 9.4, supply chains have often been push driven. Manufacturers designed new products in line with their perceptions of customer preference and consumer demand. These products would be made in-house with some input from third party suppliers. Products would be marketed and sold to the customer through retailers. Across the supply chain, due to inherent logistical inefficiencies, production difficulties, variability in demand and poor forecasting techniques, stock would pile up and all parties would experience the costly frustrations of delays and lengthy lead times.

More recently, and particularly through the pressure of major retailers, but also within sectors such as healthcare, there has been a change from this push driven supply chain towards a more a pull driven demand chain. In this way, changes to product flow become more visible to supply chain participants concurrently as the events causing the change occur.

So, for example, with efficient consumer response, unusually high unplanned demand at a customer, retail or hospital location is immediately communicated via the

Case Study:
US Healthcare
Applying efficient consumer response to the healthcare supply chain

The Efficient Healthcare Consumer Response (EHCR) coalition comprises five associations: the American Society for Health Care Materials Management, the Health Industry Business Communications Council, the Health Industry Distributors Association, the National Wholesale Druggists' Association and the Uniform Code Council. Their pilot studies indicate that a staggering $11 billion in annual savings are readily available from a spend of $23 billion.

These will come from the adoption of the 'quick response' and 'efficient consumer response' strategies more usually found in the mass retail sector. Three linked initiatives are proposed:

1. **Efficient product movement**: requiring radically revamped inventory management control systems, EDI transactions, automatic capture of demand data and the establish-

ment of continuous replenishment processes. Savings target: $6.7 billion.

2. **Efficient order management**: utilizing electronic customer, contract, product and pricing identification, electronic funds transfer, shared databases and activity based costing performance measures. Savings target: $1.7 billion.

3. **Efficient information sharing**: involving implementation of codification standards, use of value added networks and point-of-use data capture. Savings target: $2.6 billion.

It appears that almost half of the supply chain costs could be avoided or eliminated. Making the changes happen now calls for process and technology change, harnessed by committed management.

internet or proprietory EDI to the distribution centres, production facilities, material suppliers and transportation providers so that plans and schedules can be adjusted automatically and simultaneously across the complete supply chain. Action can then be taken to meet the new levels of demand quickly, with minimum cost and, thus, profitably for all the participants.

The need for a driving vision of change

The electronic supply chain does not exist on its own. When any business or government agency decides to trade electronically there will be a need to develop the technologies, challenge existing processes and create an agreed, standardized and integrated architecture. This needs a vision of how to apply communications and information exchange processes across complete supply chains.

Such an extended enterprise will usually be attained through a number of sequential phases. Firstly, implement and apply EDI and internet technologies. Do so with your in-house operations and a small number of close trading parties. Then, in a second phase, begin to scrutinize the complete supply chain and consider the options available for radical streamlining and close integration of demand driven processes. Implement your preferred improvements.

Clearly, many elements within the supply chain will be impacted by the use of electronic commerce and the application of the rapidly developing technologies for data transfer and information management. It is vital, however, that your executive team look beyond these near term opportunities. The real potential for securing business advantage will be realized through the creation of new markets and the delivery of innovative products or services that cannot be replicated by competitors. Ensure that this requirement is the real driver of change.

'A complex system that works is invariably found to have evolved from a simple system that worked. A complex system designed from scratch never works, and cannot be made to work. You have to start over, beginning with a working system.' John Gall, 'Systemantics'.

The electronic supply chain action checklist

Activities to launch straight away

1. Determine the short-term initiatives in electronic commerce that will secure incremental value rapidly. Execute these initiatives immediately.
2. Use these initial initiatives to promote in-house learning and build capability. Involve close trading partners in this exercise.
3. Benchmark best practice in efficient consumer response. Take a look at what your competitors are doing. Assess the scope for operational improvement.
4. Set 3:1 year goals for the application of efficient product movement, efficient order management and efficient order sharing.

Initiatives to make a significant difference

1. Diagnose the full potential of electronic commerce on your competitors, suppliers, products and customers.
2. Develop an information strategy that identifies how electronic data access, capture and transfer can become a critical asset for your business.
3. Ensure that this strategic vision covers both internal and external information. It needs to be focused on points of entry into new markets.
4. Reassess the role and positioning of your company in its value chain. Identify how you can channel sales to different markets through electronic commerce.

CHAPTER TEN

Governance, ethics and supply sustainability

Overview

1. Corporate governance and ethical integrity
2. Social commitment and ethical auditing
3. Reducing environmental impact
4. Responsible supply
5. Dealing with manipulation in supply chains
6. Countervailing measures for anti-competitive behaviour
7. Remedies for supply collusion and monopolies

The Bottom Line

Everyone in an organization needs to know the difference between acceptable and unacceptable commercial, social and environmental practice. Without such precision in ethical stance, the risk of a company severely damaging its reputation is unacceptably high. This can wreak havoc on brands, morale and shareholder value. Indeed, it can undermine the very sustainability of the business.

Corporate governance and ethical integrity

Two concepts dominate thinking in this area. Stakeholder theory dates back to 1937 when Ronald Coase, the British born Nobel prize-winning economist, argued that companies operated by balancing the competing claims of shareholders, customers, workers, creditors and the local community. It has become increasingly in vogue within political circles and more generally in society, because of a deepening concern that companies have gone too far in satisfying the needs of just one interest group: their shareholders. The essence of the concept is that economic success, within both business and countries, depends not so much upon the pursuit of self-interest but rather on trust, co-operation and the existence of shared and inclusive values. In this context, as is seen in Figure 10.1, a prime role of the board of a company is to accept fully its responsibility for the framing of an appropriate regime of corporate governance; one that maps out the connections between business and societal values, commercial trading principles and ethical practices.

Figure 10.1

The board needs to ensure that corporate governance, ethical integrity and social responsibility are addressed across the company

Define the values and trading principles	Develop and apply ethical policies	Communicate and involve all relevant stakeholders	Audit, monitor and scrutinize implementation
• Produce outline values statements within the board. • Allocate board roles and responsibilities. • Involve independent non-executives.	• Produce a framework statement on required practices. • Task senior management and specialists to produce the detail. • Provide a board challenge before formalization.	• Go public to shareholders and regulatory bodies. • Publish and circulate details to employees and suppliers. • Set up task groups to examine specialist areas.	• Conduct annual audit of commercial integrity. • Incorporate findings within internal training programmes. • Focus on the unresolved issues and ambiguities.

The dilemma with this thinking, however, is that it fails to address how a stakeholder corporation will take decisions on the products to make or services to provide, for which markets, or by what production methods. Equally, it is of little value in determining what to charge customers or how to raise the capital needed to sustain its business. Indeed, one of its most trenchant critics, Elaine Sternberg, has said that 'the socially responsible business is a loose cannon, and a menace to itself and others'. The alternative concept, therefore, is that the appropriate stance for an ethical organization is the vigorous pursuit of long-term

'Ethics must begin at the top of an organization. It is a leadership issue and the chief executive must set the example.'
Edward L. Hennessy, CEO, Allied Signal.

Case Study:
Wickes
The need for governance, transparency and board controls on executives

Wickes is a well established and sizeable do-it-yourself building products company in the UK.

It was also a business prepared to ramp profits by distorting its balance sheet through the incorrect booking of supplier rebates which were often linked to unrealistic volume targets. Indeed, some commercial arrangements were being run solely to generate rebates and profit contribu-tions in one year at the expense of later years. There was a failure of the group's senior management controls to prevent it from occurring.

As a result, profits were overstated by £51 million between 1992 and 1996 at the group's main DIY retailing subsidiary. This accounting scam centred on the purchasing department. It cost the jobs of the Chairman and the Finance Director.

shareholder or owner value. Unfortunately, this can easily lead to commercial malpractice and untrammelled greed. The Wickes case study is an unusually public illustration of such pursuit but one without a corresponding framework of transparency, governance and the required scrutiny of executive decision making.

The missing element is some form of 'distributive justice'. This is defined as the allocation of reward in proportion to the contributions made in pursuit of corporate purpose, plus 'ordinary decency' involving acting ethically, properly and fairly while refraining from exploitation, coercion or similarly unacceptable behaviour. Many executives talk about stakeholders while actually concentrating on shareholders. Clearly, commercial life is often regarded as being hedged around with choices between ethical integrity and profits. However, throughout this chapter we will argue that it makes sense to regard ethics, social responsibility and supply chain sustainability through good environmental policies as eminently sound business practice. Furthermore, a company's reputation with customers and the general public is a critical asset.

Social commitment and ethical auditing

'A business must have a conscience as well as a counting house.' Sir Montague Burton, Founder, Burton Group.

As businesses become more global, and access to supply chains virtually unrestricted (as can be seen in Chapter Nine on the use of electronic commerce), it becomes more important that companies are seen to be good corporate citizens. Many are investing significant amounts of money on community projects, charitable activities or corporate sponsorship as a means of promoting, or creating, positive perceptions of their social values. In some cases, of course, this is mere window dressing, but in other instances it is a genuine attempt at aiding the communities that they serve.

Equally, a number of pioneering organizations are taking the initiative on auditing their commercial practices within the context of socially defined perspectives of acceptable behaviour. This approach, ethical auditing, is a way of putting their espoused mission statements to the test. The starting point is the values that a company asserts it is trying to achieve in its market place and across its supply chains. It can either be adopted from a narrowly defined perspective of locating and assessing specific areas for improvement or it can become a highly visible strand of a broader, more open dialogue between companies and their many stakeholders.

So far, only a small number of companies have embarked on the approach. Cynics will respond that companies only become interested in corporate and social responsibility when these become serious public concerns. As can be seen in the Marks & Spencer case study, that is a partial interpretation of the importance which many corporations place on both the application of ethical sourcing and the value of their reputations in the customer market place.

Loss of reputation is potentially business threatening. It can wreak havoc on brand and stock value. Regard it and defend it as a critical asset.

Equally, however, the vitriolic criticism of Nike and Shell demonstrates very strongly that companies can no

---

Case Study:

Marks & Spencer
Immediate response to potential supply chain vulnerability

Marks & Spencer (M&S) is the most successful retailer in the UK, and in the top league worldwide. It enjoys a particularly close relationship with its predominantly middle class customers.

In January 1996 a TV channel, Granada, in their 'World in Action' programme, made a series of allegations that M&S was knowingly and deliberately exploiting child labour to boost profits and had deliberately misled customers by labelling their St. Michael branded products with incorrect country-of-origin labels.

M&S's response was immediate. It set up a 'hit squad' to audit its suppliers. Random visits were undertaken to foreign factories to make absolutely sure none of them were employing under-age workers. They wrote to suppliers and reminded them of the strict service obligations of working with M&S. All of their 330,000 shareholders and 4 million charge card holders were notified to deny the allegations. Finally, it circulated 3,500 'letter from the board' posters for display in the stores.

This £1 million plus action was highly effective, if expensive, damage limitation from a company that prides itself on its reputation for quality and integrity. How would your company stand up to similar exposure?

---

longer afford to ignore the way in which their commercial actions are perceived. Nike has been dogged by allegations over subsistence pay rates, worker intimidation and the use of child labour; so much so, that it had to resort to sweeping defensive measures involving the termination of a number of supply relationships, the introduction of a system of penalties for supplier factories that did not meet all of the company's standards, and an external independent survey of conditions in factories abroad.

A global framework for ethical auditing

'Only if entrepreneurs offer constructive solutions to important societal problems in an ethically acceptable way will they enjoy freedom of action.'
Klaus M. Leisinger, Director, Ciba Geigy Ltd.

Some of the world's largest companies have decided to support a new, verifiable code of conduct, Social Accountability 8000, in response to mounting consumer concern and criticism of the exploitative conditions under which the goods they sell are produced in certain countries. Among the well-known companies are firms such as Sainsbury's, Avon, Reebok, Toys R Us and The Body Shop. SA8000 has been developed by the Council on Economic Priorities, a US public interest group, to provide a global reference point along similar lines to the widely accepted commercial quality standard ISO9000. The code covers the key issues of child employment, forced labour, health and safety, trade union rights, discrimination, discipline, working hours and pay. Its strength comes from its worldwide applicability and its adoption of commercial sanctions. Earlier initiatives, under the aegis of the International Labour Organisation and the United Nations, had failed due to a reluctance to apply financial penalties. Furthermore, independent practices that had been adopted by a few enlightened firms in isolation from other companies had actually raised the burden on some producers. Different codes of conduct being applied by different customers and using different monitoring methods were all adding to the costs of supply chain compliance.

The new approach will ensure that no two companies using the same supplier will need to invest in two separate ethical audits. Any company which adopts the code has to agree to being independently inspected to see whether it is abiding by the conditions laid down. Verification will be conducted by independent commercial organizations to whom companies will pay a fee for certification that they comply with the code. Toys R Us, for example, which supplies a fifth of the US toy market, now requires all of its 5,000 global suppliers to be certified in this way.

Reducing environmental impact

Managing the environment illustrates the balance between firms pursuing goals that are driven solely by concern for shareholders and their obligations to broader groups such as customers and the general public. More and more companies are developing group-wide, consistent policies with regard to the environment and are increasingly prepared to address the issues associated with sustainable business development. This is clearly in response to a number of factors; the legislative environment, market characteristics, changing consumer patterns and values, the availability of more sophisticated manufacturing techniques and the power of retailers to impose supply chain change.

There is still much inertia within the supply chain. Driving change and environmental improvement, rather than its being imposed through legislation, often requires pressure from a dominant firm within the chain. Retailers are providing this in many countries.

Without doubt there has been a crucial contribution in the form of legislation. It is now fierce in some countries such as Germany where, for example, the Law for the Reduction and Avoidance of Packaging Waste 1990 has required companies to accept responsibility for the disposal of the packaging that they supply with a product. As an illustration, if a company supplies a refrigerator packed in plastic and cardboard for transit protection, then it must remove the packaging when it is delivered or make suitable arrangements for its collection. Clearly, a stricter legislative regime is gaining momentum worldwide. Regulation will get tougher. Business will increasingly be compelled to make greater investment in environmentally friendly trade practices.

Delivering value to the customer

The legislation is very much a response to growing public concern for environmental matters. Consumer awareness of such issues has begun to affect shopping habits and, in turn, product choice. This has prompted the need for visible and timely initiatives on the part of manufacturers and suppliers. There are distinct parallels here with lean thinking and the concept of 'more from less'. The goal is to develop and deliver a value proposition to the customer that triggers a positive environmental response and a clear propensity to purchase. Part of the proposition is that the performance of a product can be improved by using fewer resources and by generating less waste.

Responsible supply and environmental impact

A number of practical and direct interventions, designed to minimize environmental impact, are being made in many sectors. The following are drawn from the retail supply chain:

■ develop corporate wide and supply chain specific policies towards the environment;

Case Study:
B&Q
Environmental policy and supplier management

B&Q is a major UK 'do-it-yourself' and home improvement retailer. Since 1990 they have put in place a planned programme to reduce the environmental impact of every product that they sell.

In 1991 it became B&Q company policy for all of their 600 suppliers to have an environmental policy, backed up by an action plan. By mid-1994, over 90% of suppliers had such a policy.

Building on that progress, from 1995 B&Q launched a supplier assess-ment programme called QUEST, ensuring that quality and environmental performance are given appropriate coverage. QUEST stands for Quality, Ethics, Safety and Treatment of products, and measures suppliers on ten key quality or environmental principles.

Suppliers not meeting the required performance against QUEST do not have any new products listed by B&Q until they have addressed the problem concerned. Continued inaction results in the company being de-listed.

■ develop environmental performance indicators and set specific targets for improvement;
■ commission and publish the findings of environmental audits on energy reduction, raw materials sourcing, packaging, distribution, recycling and pollution;
■ design environmental sustainability into the product

and re-engineer upstream product development processes and specifications to achieve this;

- agree modular and standardized approaches across a complete supply chain, e.g. common storage systems, joint vehicle utilization, pooled warehousing and stacking operations, shared trays and pallet ownership;
- design for disassembly, dismantling and recycling as part of the total product value proposition;
- assess environmental life cycle across sourcing, production, distribution, consumption, disposal and recycling;
- reduce environmental impact through a lean approach, e.g. less raw material usage, less virgin raw material use, less energy usage, fewer emissions, less waste going into final disposal;
- reduce the level of packaging taken home by consumers at source, e.g. light weighting, thin walling, redesign to reduce material use;
- reduce packaging used to protect goods during distribution, e.g. returnable transit packaging;
- encourage recycling initiatives in local communities;
- provide channels for customer reaction and redress, including prompt product alerts and recalls.

'Conducting your business in a socially responsible way is good business. It means that you can attract better employees and that customers will know what you stand for and like you for it.'
Anthony Burns, CEO, Ryder Systems.

Taking the initiative across the supply chain

In the past, many businesses operated with scant regard to the environment. They simply pursued damaging practices until they were caught. There is now much greater awareness of the need for pre-emptive, preventative action both from individual companies and across the complete supply chain. Most organizations now realize that one of the most effective means of dealing with a particular environmental problem is to avoid creating it. This is often best addressed by optimizing resources employed through a total supply chain. This can eliminate wasteful use of materials and energy, and minimizes emissions into air and water. However, in common with so many supply chain issues, this requires a preparedness to address both internal operational difficulties and sectoral reluctance to make changes.

'The strength of commitment to a high level of ethical business behaviour has deteriorated almost in direct proportion to declining societal values.' Robert L. Koch, Vice President Human Resources, Bally of Switzerland.

Dealing with manipulation of supply chains

We saw in Chapter Two that active market management is a crucial feature of any successful business. An ethical issue that needs to be addressed, however, is the appropriate executive response to questionable or even illegal collusion between players in the supply chain striving to achieve that success. This is particularly the case in the context of cartels and price fixing, which are examined below, but it applies equally to other types of collusion, including:

- officially sanctioned and regulated market places;
- vertically integrated supply chains;
- supply chains that compete with their end customer;
- supply chains which supply all, or the vast majority, of customers in a given market sector.

In each of these cases the constituent members of a supply chain may collude with each other against their supposed customer. It is important to understand how these different types of collusion achieve that end purpose, and then determine appropriate responses.

Recognize that cartels are common

A cartel exists when supplying firms agree to collude between themselves to carve up and share out a market. The primary objective is the fixing and/or raising of prices above the level that would naturally occur in an open, fully contested market. The activities pursued by such outright cartels are of course illegal and blatantly anti-competitive. Furthermore, they are directly damaging to the purchasers of goods and services, since they limit the full delivery of value through to the end customer. There are three types of cartel and overtly anti-competitive agreements:

- **The price fixing cartel** – whereby participating firms ensure that they are all able to charge higher prices for goods or services than they would be able to achieve if they actively competed against each other. This is applied in a way that achieves common net pricing.

- **The market sharing cartel** – whereby firms agree amongst themselves which company will receive a particular contract in response to an open market tender to bid.
- **The market restricting cartel** – whereby dominant players agree common action, on pricing or supply, to prevent the entrance of new market competitors.

The examples of Bouygues and Archer Daniels Midland are fairly typical. Such collusion is most prevalent in markets where available capacity is restricted in some way. It often reflects geographical problems, physical locational issues, high barriers to entry and considerable capital costs of

---

Case Study:

Bouygues

Corruption in the French construction sector

Most staff working in the commercial area will have encountered anti-competitive practices, and even corruption. Unfortunately, the legal processes to expose such distortions in the market place are needlessly bureaucratic and long winded. The work of the French Competition Council, which was established in 1987, illustrates this. The Bouygues case is one of the few concerted drives against cartels in Europe. However, other sectors such as telecommunications and the electricity industry are now also under review.

In 1996, record fines of FFr388 million were levied on the construction industry for price fixing in public sector projects worth over FFr10 billion. Thirty six companies had been accused of creating cartels for contracts ranging from the TGV high speed railway to the new Normandy suspension bridge over the Seine. The main culprits were the huge French conglomerate Bouygues, which was fined FFr148.7 million; Enterprise Industrielle and Campenon Bernard, who were each fined more than FFr30 million; and Quillery and Spie Batignolles, who faced fines of over FFr20 million. Criminal corruption charges were also considered.

---

supply. In these circumstances, particularly where profit margins are very dependent on the level of capacity utilization, it will be in the producer's interests to minimize fluctuations in demand and create a stable pattern of supply. This delivers acceptable margin management when capacity loading is secured through fairly won contracts. It is when this activity shifts from sensible operational planning into explicit agreements with competitors on the rigging of the market that such practices become unacceptable.

Case Study:
Archer Daniels Midland
Price fixing and collusive behaviour in the US foods sector

In 1996 the US Justice Department announced that its investigation into alleged price-fixing by the international food company ADM had been boosted by plea agreements with three of ADM's rivals in the $600 million lysine market.

ADM, based in Decatur, Illinois, produces about 47% of the world's lysine. In 1994, an ADM employee became an undercover agent for the FBI, making audio and video tapes of meetings with competitors and conversations between ADM executives.

One New Jersey–South Korean and two Japanese companies have now admitted that they conspired to fix prices to eliminate competition and allocate sales in the market for lysine, an amino acid used as a feed additive to enhance growth in livestock.

ADM and its rivals agreed in July 1996 to pay $45 million to lysine customers to settle a civil anti-trust suit.

In its first action against international cartel activity in the food and feed additive industry, the Justice Department stated that 'it sends a message to the entire world that collusive behaviour that harms US consumers will not be tolerated'.

Unacceptable carving up of the market

'We don't sit down and consider whether decisions may be fair or not. We try and find out how we can make people fly in our airplanes rather than other people's.' Robert Ayling, CEO, British Airways.

Participating companies in a cartel agree amongst themselves who should receive a particular contract and its preferred terms. Despite the fact that such overt rigging of a competitive bid is illegal, and is usually actionable as criminal fraud, it is very common in certain sectors and countries. Clearly, the commercial goal of an effective tendering or bidding process is the creation of true competition and the selection of the most suitable supplier, evaluated against balanced criteria of cost, value and risk. In a market sharing cartel, potential suppliers disrupt and distort that process through pre-agreement amongst themselves on the nature and detail of their bid responses to the contract awarding purchaser. This is done by:

- **bid suppression**, i.e. where a number of 'competing' companies who might have been expected to bid, do not do so or decide to withdraw their bids;
- **complementary bidding**, i.e. where 'competing' companies agree in advance to put forward bids that are demonstrably uncompetitive on price, and which will, therefore, be rejected. The contract is then awarded to another member of the cartel;
- **bid rotation**, i.e. where 'competing' companies submit bids but take turns at being the lowest and winning bidder.

'People of the same trade seldom meet together, even for merriment and diversion, but the conversation ends in a conspiracy against the public, or in some contrivance to raise prices.' Adam Smith, 'The Wealth of Nations'.

Such collusive market manipulation is designed to remove competition ahead of contracts being awarded. Price fixing, on the other hand, is common throughout the whole life cycle of the contracting process. It may involve the cartel in agreeing remarkably similar levels of volume discounts, payment terms and base prices. Not surprisingly, price increases to customers tend to be imposed by cartel members with almost military precision and timing.

Other common forms of supply chain collusion

As was emphasized earlier in the chapter, there are many other forms of collusion more subtle than mere cartels. A second type occurs in officially regulated market places when companies operating within such markets decide to shelter behind the regulations to avoid competing with one another. For example, in the early stages of the privatization of the UK electricity market, many of the regional electricity companies indicated to their customers that certain pricing elements would have to remain fixed in order to comply with specific regulatory requirements such as fossil fuel levies. There was, in fact, much more price flexibility than was implied.

Collusion also occurs within markets that are serviced by a totally vertically integrated supply chain where all of

It is naive to believe that companies only focus on to customer delight. Many pursue collusive strategies that maximize profit at the expense of their customers. But it is equally naive to ignore the countervailing measures that develop to curtail such practice.

the constituent links are owned by a single parent company. Experience demonstrates that these are far less likely to be customer–driven than ones in which the supply links are owned by different organizations. In the latter case, commercial pressures will usually ensure that at least one link will adopt a customer focused approach. This in turn can then be used to drive similar behaviour with the other links in the chain. However, in the vertically integrated chain, collusion may readily occur to ensure that maximum value is appropriated and retained within the chain for the parent company. Much less value is then delivered through to the customer. Examples can readily be found within mineral extraction and processing sectors.

A fourth type of collusion is found when a supply chain acts as a competitor to its own prime customer. For example, tier one suppliers in the automotive sector may supply a component to the auto assembler which they also sell in the aftermarket under a proprietary banner brand

Figure 10.2

Collusive activity and cartel formation are a feature of many markets. Strengthen commercial supply chain practice to resist it

Anti-Competitive Behaviour	Countervailing Bid Measures
Price fixing and non-competitive bidding	• Benchmark prices with cost synthesis and in-house data. • Require bids to be broken down into detailed cost data. • Keep records of bids and plot price trends.
Collusion between competing firms	• Make non-collusion a fundamental contract term. • Insert non-collusion warranties into contracts. • Require signed declarations of non-collusion. • Use liquidated damages/pre-estimates of loss clauses in contracts.
Upstream and downstream supplier manipulation	• Require main contractors to adopt a competitive sourcing process with sub-contractors. • Seek detailed information from bidders about subsidiaries and associated companies.
Restricting competition in an open market	• Break a project down into smaller parts and bid them out. • Review entry criteria to approved supplier lists. • Relax restrictions and required minimum bid entry qualifications. • Exclude companies which regularly submit high bids.

that has been packaged by their own sub-contract suppliers. When this happens suppliers are direct competitors of the aftermarket operations of the major manufacturers. This readily influences the decisions that determine how they compete for the original equipment orders.

A final type of collusion against the end consumer is found in the retail industry. Many suppliers to supermarket outlets supply all of the major grocery chains. If they enhance value to only one of their customers, it can lead to cannibalization of sales volumes from other outlets. This easily becomes a zero sum end game for these companies. In such circumstances suppliers may seek to avoid providing new levels of added value, such as product innovation or creative ideas on packaging, until it is absolutely demanded of them by their supermarket customers.

Remedies for supply collusion and monopolies

A number of specific interventions, designed to create fair competition within bidding procedures, have been described in Figure 10.2. Other broader strategies, to be applied in collusive and monopolistic markets, include:

- focusing on the weak link in the cartel;
- understanding the supply market drivers;
- locating the pressure points for change;
- forming a consortium with other non-competing companies to build market place leverage;
- developing new suppliers;
- using suppliers, possessing the required capabilities, from other sectors;
- investing capital into such programmes of supplier development;
- redesigning the product to avoid restricted supply;
- identifying ownership and trading links between 'competing' suppliers;
- global and transnational sourcing;
- circulating unfavourable press reports;
- using the legislation and regulatory power.

Effective sourcing and commercial practice should relish the challenge of anti-competitive behaviour in collusive or monopolistic supply markets. Focus on this as a potential opportunity for competitive advantage. If your firm can secure a preferential position by breaking the cartel, then it's your gain, compared to other companies who just accept the status quo.

Governance, ethics and supply chain sustainability – action checklist

Activities to launch straight away

1. Sponsor an integrity audit of the company's commercial practices to assess vulnerability and potential corruption.
2. Introduce systems and controls to minimize exposure to corporate fraud and malpractice.
3. Develop sourcing strategies and tighten up bid procedures to deal with cartels, price fixing and monopolies.
4. Conduct a social and environmental audit.
5. Produce an ethical policy and a statement of required standards of business conduct.
6. Develop a common business vocabulary on what is meant by value, ethics and supply sustainability.
7. Instigate the required training and coaching programmes and cascade them down through the business.

Initiatives to make a significant difference

1. Pay considerable attention to how the company's name and reputation are presented to, and rated by, the media, customers and shareholders.
2. Prepare the appropriate contingency plans that may be required to defend reputation if it comes under attack.
3. Appoint a board director with specific responsibility to look after the intangible elements in the company's name and brand profile.
4. Assess the upstream impact of new product development processes on downstream environmental waste and pollution.
5. Sponsor cross supply chain initiatives, in conjunction with other companies, to remove waste and inefficiency.
6. Define and then develop an appropriate level of ethical competence inside the organization.
7. Role model the required leadership behaviours.

CHAPTER ELEVEN

Measurement and baselining

Overview

1. Integrating total corporate performance and the supply chain
2. Performance metrics and organizational level
3. Activity outcomes vs. process drivers
4. Harnessing the motivational power of measurement
5. Measuring the effectiveness of measurement
6. The value of qualitative measures
7. The need for process measurement
8. Using baselining and benchmarking

The Bottom Line

Supply chain measurement has a pivotal role in transformational change. It builds commitment, motivates teams and generates forward momentum. Embedding an effective measurement scheme into the culture of a business calls for sustained executive challenge. It requires the restructuring of performance management processes.

'I think it is an immutable law in business that words are words, explanations are explanations, promises are promises — but only performance is reality.' Harold Geneen on 'managing'.

Measuring total corporate performance

From the earliest times of business, measurement has been regarded as a classic tool of management.

Failure to measure is regarded as being both inappropriate and an indication of a lack of suitable organizational control. Management consultancies vie with each other to develop new measures relevant to the gauging of company performance. Financial analysts continually assess the appropriateness of measures aimed at assessing shareholder value. The financial community has been debating at length over whether total shareholder return, economic value added, market value added, earnings per share, return on sales, return on capital employed or return on net assets are the more effective guides to corporate performance. Quite rightly, this debate has gained considerable attention amongst the shareholder, fund management and senior executive community. One of the core themes of this chapter, therefore, is that supply chain measurement must integrate with, and have specific links to, these measures of corporate performance. (A glossary of these terms is provided at the end of the chapter.)

The criticality of measurement

From the perspective of the chief executive, measurement is about calibrating effectively the net effect of the execution of a wide array of inter-related activities, business strategies and operational initiatives throughout the organization.

These measures need to provide valuable, valid and timely information on the direction and relative strengths of value delivery that the business is providing to its stakeholders. They must enable shareholders and senior management to assess and review performance. Results against previously set targets have to be evaluated. New goals need to be articulated with regard to requirements for enhanced value delivery to customers.

A range of supply chain performance metrics are available. They serve different purposes at different organizational levels

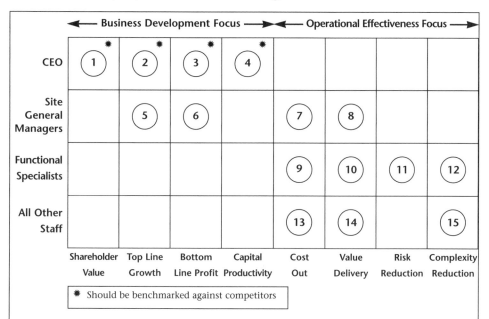

	◄── Business Development Focus ──►◄── Operational Effectiveness Focus ──►							
CEO	①✳	②✳	③✳	④✳				
Site General Managers		⑤	⑥		⑦	⑧		
Functional Specialists					⑨	⑩	⑪	⑫
All Other Staff					⑬	⑭		⑮
	Shareholder Value	Top Line Growth	Bottom Line Profit	Capital Productivity	Cost Out	Value Delivery	Risk Reduction	Complexity Reduction

✳ Should be benchmarked against competitors

Performance Metrics to be Applied Across the Supply Chain

1 Total shareholder return (TSR), economic value added (EVA) and earnings per share (EPS) address both capital appreciation and revenue stream issues for shareholders.

2 Return on sales (ROS), i.e. incremental sales of the same 'value' as existing sales.

3 Operating profit before tax and exceptionals, i.e. underlying profit performance.

4 Return on capital employed and return on net assets. Which measure is used depends upon whether assets are largely tangible or intangible.

5 Ratio of existing business to new business, i.e. a focus on retention and cost of new sales.

6 Percentage gross margin, i.e. allows a focus on sales growth and the cost of it.

7 Year-on-year change in standards, i.e. annualized change in cost base, including purchase price variance during the year.

8 Operating costs, i.e. staff to manage the supply chain, e.g. reduced goods inwards inspection; consignment stocking; smaller supply base/ fewer suppliers.

9 Zero based measurement (ZBM), i.e. focus on purchasing performance.

10 Number of continuous improvement agreements in place; number of suppliers co-located; and the number of suppliers involved in target costing.

11 Percentage of vulnerable items dual approved with replacement suppliers.

12 Number of active suppliers, together with clear profiling of their capabilities.

13 Reducing or static budgets, i.e. for marketing/ engineering.

14 Involvement in supplier development teams and involvement of suppliers at early stages of new product development.

15 Reduction in number of stock-keeping units (SKUs) and clearly mapped roles and responsibilities.

'We have always understood and measured our margins with rigour, but before the introduction of ZBM we had no handle on a key contributor – buyer performance. Now we target purchasing for specific contributions to margin enhancement.' Colin Billiet, Group CEO, domnick hunter plc.

A fundamental issue in measurement, though, is that this process does not necessarily provide any insight at all into how an organization actually achieves its required goals. This is because many systems are only measuring outcomes or symptoms. They are not addressing the underlying causes. This is illustrated in Figure 11.2.

This approach may be acceptable at the level of total measurement of organizational performance. Such aggregated outputs will indeed reflect the interconnections and interrelatedness of a huge array of business interventions. What is of more concern, though, is the way in which at lower levels within many organizations such symptomatic measurement remains the dominant methodology.

The case study on aircraft repair and maintenance typifies how many businesses frequently apply inappropriate and confused systems of supply chain measurement.

Figure 11.2

Shareholder value is delivered through a value chain of interconnected activities. Address the causative factors, not the effects

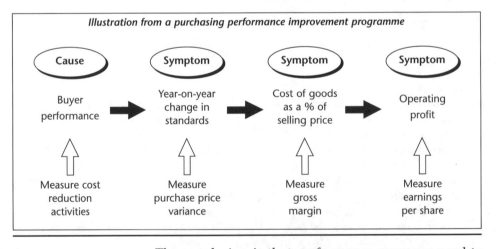

The conclusion is that performance measures need to be segmented into those that can examine:

- **activity outcomes**, i.e. the symptoms or indicators of effective performance; and
- **business process drivers**, i.e. the causative factors of successful supply chain performance.

We will use purchasing cost management to illustrate the principal differences between these two approaches. A typical example is of the need for measurement segmentation to assess purchasing effectiveness appropriately. This is

Case Study:
Sector: Aircraft Operation (Repair and Maintenance)
Measuring outputs of performance (deliverables) rather than inputs (activities)

The classic performance measure used amongst aircraft operators is the AOG (Aircraft on the Ground). Equally, its corollary, percentage utilization of the aircraft, is regularly applied.

Clearly, the consequential losses inherent in failing to have the components necessary to service or repair an aircraft, and return it to operations, can be huge. In such circumstances the management fixation with AOGs is understandable.

What is less acceptable, though, is why this utilization focus should result in such a preponderance of input measures applied to the logistics operations of aircraft operators. These usually take the form of process measures such as:

- lead time to action a requisition to order;
- number of orders placed within lead times;
- number of aircraft declared AOG or targeted to be AOG in seven days.

Such input measures are clearly designed to identify areas where operational activities can be improved. The assumption is that targeting in this way

will lead to an improvement in AOGs. While there can be some benefit in a measure of this nature, a more powerful approach is to use output measures that drive activities which are clearly focused on AOG prevention.

One example will illustrate this. AOG data should be segmented and measured through categories such as:

- AOGs that can be resolved through cannibalization of other aircraft;
- AOGs resulting from routine service operations;
- AOGs resulting from unforecast repair activity;
- AOGs created by supplier failure to perform to standard delivery lead time.

Such measures will prompt a logistics operation to focus improvements on to the most appropriate areas such as forecasting, inventory management techniques and the extraction of enhanced performance/value improvement from suppliers. A measurement system applied in this manner will prevent all but the most exceptional AOGs.

an area where there are a number of differing views on the subject of cost performance. The most frequent measures employed are purchase price variance (PPV), zero based purchase price variance (ZBPPV) and zero based measurement (ZBM). It is important to note that while these measures are sometimes regarded as alternative methodologies, they are, in practice, measuring very different outputs. Figure 11.3 highlights the main features of each measure.

Figure 11.3

A number of cost measurement options are readily available. Focus more on how you will use the outputs than on their calculation

	Purchase Price Variance (PPV)	Zero Based Purchase Price Variance (ZBPPV)	Zero Based Measurement (ZBM)
Definition of Cost Movement	• Uses pre-set standard prices • Uses actual volumes	• Uses previous price paid • Uses actual volumes consumed each month	• Uses previous price paid • Uses fixed annual volumes, usually from budget
Focus of Purchasing Activity	• Conditioning by supplier • Standard setting • Cost movement reporting • Budget targeting • Variance analysis, e.g. price, volume, financial impact	• Conditioning of suppliers • Achievement of net PPV target *not* individual buyer targets and performance • Reconciliation of PPV to ZBM	• Conditioning of suppliers • Cost forecasting, cost reduction and cost containment • Prioritization of activity • Individual objective setting • Cost movement reporting by exception only • Net reduction targeting
Systems Implications	• Impossible without integration into main system	• Impossible without integration into main system	• Expenditure handled simply or within the financial system
Impact on Purchasing	• Budget mentality • Acceptance of year-on-year increases	• Awareness of *all* increases • Variance analysis is simplified	• Cost down mentality • Focuses buyers on *all* cost movements
Benefit to the Business	• Management of profit margin • Risk management	• Allows easy reconciliation of ZBM and PPV • Risk management	• Provides a measure of buyer performance • Gives focus for business review

© ADR International Purchasing Consultants.

Purchase price variance is a measure of an outcome. It is the financial impact on the business of buyer activity. Zero based measurement is attempting to assess purchasing performance in terms of the underlying drivers. This is particularly relevant in the context of the goals and business expectations that should have been set for a buying team in terms of their cost management activities.

It is certainly possible to improve performance using symptomatic measures such as   purchase price variance. This is usually achieved through focused review and action planning. It is less effective than applying a similar team development process, but one incorporating measures that are directly and closely connected with performance.

Attempting to improve a symptomatic measure of purchasing performance is unlikely to impact the initial causative factor. It will be more difficult than measuring and acting on the prime cause itself. Furthermore, only if a measure accurately pinpoints the reasons for a particular set of performance circumstances can reward, sanctions and improvement activities such as training and individual coaching be precisely targeted.

Clearly, the selection of appropriate measures of performance requires close executive scrutiny. In particular, the focus of such a review should be on a thorough examination of the reasoning behind why a particular measure needs to be selected.

Too many organizations have adopted inappropriate measures of supply chain performance. The need is to select measures that truly address the causes of superior business performance.

- Is it to measure symptoms, and therefore reliably forecast future business performance?
- Is it to examine the root causes, address the need for direct interventions into the business to improve performance?

This differentiation is crucial. Organizations that only use symptomatic measures are unlikely to achieve transformational or breakthrough change. The measures that they have selected will tend to constrain their performance. The likelihood is that only incremental improvement in results will be achieved. Executives need to be prepared to scrutinize and challenge the basis of such measurement. This is one of the most important steps in ensuring that any measurement system becomes a real 'engine' of business development and operational improvement.

Specifying the measurement matrix

As with any other area of business activity, measurement must be thoroughly planned if its value is to be optimized.

Across the supply chain, there will be many functional inputs. In each of these various functional areas, such as purchasing, logistics, production, quality assurance and distribution, it is essential that there is appropriately focused measurement to ensure that these functions perform their role as part of an integrated link in the value chain from supply right through to the end customer.

Case Study:

Sector: Building and Construction Products

Integrating target setting with appropriate measures of achievement

Most organizations, when they are trying to measure a specific feature or attribute, will develop a quantified target outcome. The argument applied is that such a target provides a guide as to what subsequently will be constituted as good or bad performance. Unfortunately, the problems many companies then face is that the targets they develop are:

- insufficiently flexible to reflect changing business circumstances;
- imposed from the 'top down' rather than being developed 'bottom up';
- global and general in nature rather than disaggregated and specific to the required business circumstances.

A typical illustration is from this building products company. They had set a supplier reduction target of 125 production suppliers. This had been developed from a top down analysis of their current supplier numbers. They assumed that a 40% reduction, from 208 suppliers, was reasonable and achievable.

Unfortunately, no parallel analysis had been conducted to determine the appropriate number of suppliers for each specific category of expenditure. The criteria or guiding principles for such an approach were lacking.

Progress towards the magical target of 125 became enshrined as the monthly measure of suppliers eliminated. It entrenched attitudes at both senior management and purchasing professional level. Quite quickly this resulted in decisions being taken that increased risk in critical segments of the purchased portfolio. In other areas, it reduced the organization's competitive leverage.

The conclusion is to beware crude aggregate targets. In particular, those developed from top down analysis, combined with inflexible measures of achievement, run the risk of actively impairing business performance.

A matrix of suitable measures should be completed by each functional area. A recommended approach is illustrated in Figure 11.4.

Figure 11.4

Each functional area represents one link in the supply chain. Draw up a measurement matrix that addresses the different roles

Measures Across the Supply Chain	Type of Measure	
	Symptomatic	Causal
Measures of inputs from suppliers	• Provides focus for discussion of deliverables • Facilitates constructive feedback	• Encourages respecification of deliverables • Highlights risks and opportunities
Measures of 'value added' within the business	• Records progress • Forecasts achievement	• Informs development needs analysis • Prompts appropriate target setting
Measures of process efficiency within the business	• Highlights areas where further measures are needed	• Informs resource allocation • Highlights strengths and weaknesses
Measure of outputs to customers	• Provides motivation • Publicizes/celebrates achievement	• Records achievement • Redefines achievable deliverables

It is further recommended that a matrix of this type be constructed under the sponsorship of executive management. A number of fundamental issues have to be borne in mind when determining the proposed measures:

- the constituency that will be responding to, and using, the measures;
- the role that the measures are to perform;
- their links to reward and compensation schemes;
- the type of improvement required;
- the frequency and duration of the measurement period;
- the resources required to create the measures, gather the data and respond to the outputs;
- the responsibilities for further action that will fall on the creators and the recipients of the measures.

Top executives and site general managers are much more concerned with receiving symptomatic measurement data that inform them of the overall performance of the supply chain and its contribution to revenue growth and the bottom line. They need aggregated, indicative measures rather than highly detailed operational data. Also, they will want to receive this information through readily accessible, visually graphic media. Conversely, if the measures are intended for use primarily within a specific function, such as purchasing, causal measures with a fine mesh of detail are more appropriate.

'Businesses have to simplify themselves. I think all great businesses can be understood by a five year old.' Martin Taylor, CEO, Barclays.

The top executive audience needs measures that they can quickly assimilate. They should be able to access and comprehend the measures without any need for significant insight into the technical nature of supply chain activities. Furthermore, it should allow them to apply the following interconnected elements of performance management:

- remuneration, reward and compensation schemes affecting their staff;
- celebration of success;
- feedback to front line subordinates;
- sanction or censure of ineffective behaviour;
- redefinition of roles, responsibilities and deliverables;
- selection criteria to fill key positions;
- creation of training and development plans;
- resource allocation and prioritization.

In some cases, however, it is certainly appropriate for measures to be more functionally specific, highly specialized in focus and technically more complex. These will require a greater degree of prior knowledge to extract full value from them. There are numerous occasions when this fine mesh of detail will be a precondition to facilitating one of the most important roles that many measures perform. This is the highlighting of strengths, weaknesses, opportunities and risks. Performance measures need to enable more effective planning of resource allocation and improvement activity while ensuring that business strengths are properly harnessed. Indeed, a gauge of the effectiveness of performance measurement is whether market opportunities are being realized effectively, while at the same time the effects of weaknesses or risks are being minimized or removed.

This potential for targeting improvement activity will be to no avail if either the creators of the measures, or those being measured, are unclear in their roles and responsibilities once the measurement data are available. Unfortunately, it is not unusual for senior managers to be seen religiously sitting through monthly reviews of supply chain performance data without any noticeable attempt to shape or drive higher expectations of performance in any particular given direction for designated businesses, sectors or functional groups. Occasionally, this may be the result of indolence. It is more often, however, a product of inappropriate and impenetrable measures being presented to them. Sometimes there can also be a failure in the provision by senior functional staff of the necessary guidance on appropriate roles for participants within the different types of measurement reviews. Although this can be a difficult subject to address, the behaviours that are needed to be effective in such situations should be made explicit.

Harnessing the motivational power of measurement

Senior functional staff may be inclined to use highly detailed causal measures as mechanisms to censure or apply pressure on their subordinates. This fundamentally misses the prime role and purpose of measurement. It should be a process designed to facilitate constructive improvement in staff performance and, when necessary, to identify and help structure training and development activity. Failure to use measurement in such a way rapidly negates its intention and can seriously demoralize staff.

Clearly, any measurement regime should be designed in such a way that the benefits expected from it are commensurate with the resources needed to develop it. Scoping and pre-specifying a supply chain measurement system is an essential initial planning element that should determine the following.

- What should be measured?
- How many measures are required?
- How frequently should specific activities be measured?
- Who should be involved in measurement?
- To what extent should third parties be involved?

- Who should receive details of the measures?
- What actions are required to utilize the measurement data?
- What feedback is needed on the activities pursued?
- What review period should be adopted?
- How will supply chain measures be integrated within other business systems?
- How can this be done in a seamless manner?
- What evaluation mechanisms are needed on measurement effectiveness?
- Who should sponsor the overall supply chain measurement process?

Rigorously applying such a logic chain, and responding to its conclusions, is crucially important in the construction of a measurement programme that is capable of driving business improvement. It will also ensure a much higher probability of success in securing active support across the many supply chain constituencies for the eventual implementation of the measurement regime.

All measurement schemes need to be kept under close scrutiny by top management. Seek evidence of their added value. Ensure that they are genuinely contributing to business improvement.

Measuring the effectiveness of measurement

There is a natural tendency in organizations to leave measurement schemes in place and unchallenged once they have been instituted. It should be emphasized that all schemes require regular update and amendment. In particular, causal measures often have a limited life. The goal of a performance measure is to influence and raise business expectations and aspirations. They need to drive performance improvement and behavioural change. Once you are confident that such process and behavioural change has taken place, and that it has been thoroughly embedded within the organization, then many measures can be discontinued. They may only need to be reinstated if the symptomatic measures which they are driving begin to indicate that intervention is once more necessary. Equally, if the specific value delivery being demanded by a customer no longer requires symptomatic measurement of specific attributes, then the measure should also be discontinued. Without this type of sensitivity analysis throughout the life cycle of measurement, it becomes too easy to allocate a disproportionate amount of time to a measurement regime that has probably fully met its objective.

A systematic annual review will ensure that the measurement regime remains valid and relevant, while properly reflecting the appropriate balance between the complexity of measurement, its costs and benefits. As is shown in Figure 11.5, the specific links between different types of measurement, and their strategic impact, need real consideration by top management. Such a review will help avoid the pitfall of creating a succession of sporadic, unpublicized measures with variable methodologies, each of which has been developed as a spontaneous attempt to 'fix' a particular problem, rather than being part of a well-

Figure 11.5

Measurement is structured into a hierarchy. It reflects the balance between operational improvement and business development

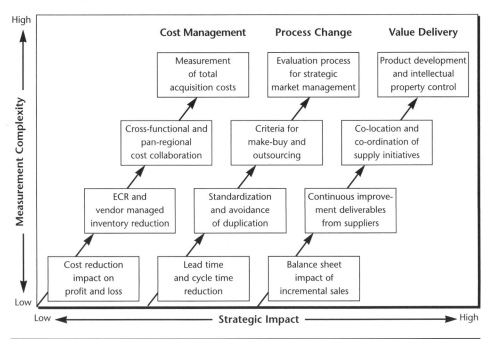

planned and integrated campaign of business improvement.

Recognize the value of qualitative measurement

It is commonly held by executives that 'what gets measured, gets managed'. This reflects the generally held view that only quantitative data are valid and credible. In fact the reality is often that 'what gets measured' is what can easily be measured. A common weakness of many measurement schemes is the relative absence of measures relating to activities or processes that cannot easily be quantified, but which may well be the primary drivers and differentiators between effective and ineffective performance. It is too easy to confer false objectivity by the mere presence of numbers. Indeed, many of the most useful supply chain measures can only be very crudely represented numerically. These include:

- value added;
- process efficiency;
- commitment to innovation;
- nature of trading relationships;
- managerial and supplier commitment;
- team cohesiveness;
- quality of leadership;
- individual competence and capability;
- collaboration between interface functions.

A balanced scorecard of supply chain measurement will address such issues. It is an important executive task to ensure that this occurs. It is too easy to allow those activities that can easily be measured, using readily available quantitative data, to dominate the decision-making process into which such data are incorporated. Finally it is important that a relatively small number of crucial measures are adopted. Be prepared to challenge the proliferation of large numbers of symptomatic measures.

Of course, qualitative measures must be well founded if they are to perform any useful role. If they are primarily symptomatic, focused on outcomes and outputs, then a crucial feature which must be present is a clear specification of the deliverables expected by the internal or external customer. One way of approaching this is to define them in terms of the anticipated value delivery. When working with internal customers in framing value based measures, a prime requirement is well developed facilitation skill to help them articulate, in sufficient detail, what they are really seeking. This is not always easy. Many customers, particularly internal ones, are notoriously vague about their requirements. For example they may happily request 'innovation from the supply base' without ever feeling a need to become more specific about the direction of that innovation and to what end it is sought.

The need for process measurement

When supply chain measurement schemes are evaluated, it is not uncommon to find a substantial emphasis on the immediate outcome. Particularly when these are beneficial to the business, little attention may be paid, or analysis made, of whether such outcomes are repeatable and sustainable. The case study from the pharmaceuticals and health care sector, however, shows how it is often necessary to dig much deeper into the operational and motivational processes behind measures of achievement if you are to understand the nature of self-sustaining change. This is a fundamental issue that any satisfactory measurement regime must address. Excellent results may be obtained simply as a result of exceptional individual commitment, or through pure good fortune. This does not provide an acceptable level of confidence in future repetition of results. On time, predictable delivery of standardized, repeatable outcomes is crucial in the management of complex long-term processes within the supply chain.

What is easy to measure, tends to get measured. Challenge and break that way of thinking. Refocus measurement on to the ways in which a company learns, adapts and applies innovative business thinking. Then test how well this is driving future strategy.

When the measurement of these processes is focused primarily on outputs, as with the pharmaceuticals company which concentrated on the number of completed source plans rather than on their quality, then no proper assessment has been made of the robustness of the process itself.

Case Study:
Sector: Pharmaceuticals and Health Care
Developing a measurement system to focus on processes and process outcomes

Measurement should not be restricted only to quantitative data. It should equally be used to monitor the effective application and enhancement of new, innovative or complex processes.

A major European company was committed to achieving closer integration of its purchasing activities through pan-regional sourcing. Substantial effort was put into the training of their staff and the requirements for development of medium to long-term strategic sourcing plans (source plans). Unfortunately, in too many instances, the plans being offered for review by senior management lacked rigour. There was insufficient evidence of systematic evaluation of the widest possible range of sourcing options.

On investigation this was found not to be an issue about staff competence. It was more fundamentally linked to the process involved. The approach lacked the necessary forums for review and appropriate challenge at several crucial stages in the development of an effective source plan.

The company's purchasing staff had been given an overview of the structure required for source planning and the timescale for developing them. But no assessment was being applied of how effectively they achieved the goals. Quite quickly both European management and their purchasing staff became disillusioned with the approach.

Process measurement was introduced to identify, and provide corrective feedback, when the source planning technique was being misapplied. The goal was to ensure that timely remedial action could be applied when necessary. The measurement interventions consisted of:

- creation of a tiered and structured set of business reviews;
- definition of the source planning facets to be presented at each review;
- explicit behavioural statements of the appropriate process outcomes at each review stage.

This approach was piloted using a 'fast track' methodology. The resulting source plans were demonstrably more rigorous and wider-ranging in scope than previous plans. They mapped out three year strategies for each category of expenditure. Furthermore, the average yield per source plan was in excess of £1 million of value improvement.

A model for the required process challenge is shown in Figure 11.6. For example, when developing sourcing strategies (source plans), sponsoring executives should ensure that the following questions are properly addressed.

Figure 11.6

Process measurement digs into the thinking, practice and behaviour of supply chain teams. Participative review and challenge are critical

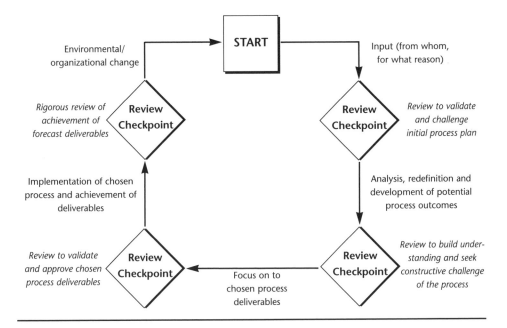

- What level of internal customer and functional challenge has taken place?
- What sources of market analysis data were accessed?
- How extensive is the range of sourcing options that have been developed?
- How rigorous and objective was the method of option selection?
- Do these options address both short term as well as longer term business needs?
- What level of risk may be inherent in the selected sourcing option?
- How far is potential risk understood and accepted by internal customers and functional management?

- How will the implementation plan be introduced into the business?
- Which functional and business constituencies need to be involved in this?
- What blocks and barriers may be encountered?
- How will these be addressed?

Do not accept a supply chain proposal, no matter how well it is presented, without a searching challenge of the fundamental thinking behind it. Ensure that teams build sufficient time in their project plans for a systematic and thorough review of the full range of strategic and operational options available to them.

All of these questions relate to qualitative evaluation of the sourcing process itself and associated organizational issues. They require a searching challenge from the executive sponsors. The need is for a readiness to get behind the planned outputs into the quality of business thinking that underpins them. As we have seen in the earlier chapters of this book, there is a particular requirement to ensure that market management interventions, for example those concerned with joint ventures and partnerships, are properly focused in this way. As an illustration, if your business were considering participation in a collaborative marketing venture of an innovative service, then you would need to consider:

- What understanding of ownership rights exist regarding legal entities, intellectual property control, infrastructural property and distribution channels?
- How far does the analysis recognize the impact of such ownership rights?
- Does the analysis assess the degrees of dependence that the supply chain may have on dominant customers or suppliers?
- Is it clear from the analysis whether the supply chain participants are collaborating or in competition with each other?
- How does this meet the specific business needs of the participants?
- Is this situation transitional and/or opportunistic and/or based on mutual gain?
- What are the implications of each of these options?
- What information and analysis has been used to form appropriate conclusions?
- What is the downside risk in the relational strategies being considered?

- How will the inevitable difficulties and conflicts in the relationships be addressed?
- Will current levels of competence and capability in the participating organizations be able to cope with this?
- If not, what is the way forward?

In our experience, insufficient consideration is given to such questions. Furthermore, in many organizations, there is no forum to ensure that robust business challenge really takes place. This is a key area for executive attention.

Create a supply chain strategy forum

Effective management of such complex processes as source planning and relational analysis clearly requires the managerial construction of appropriate checkpoints and reviews. At such points qualitative, causal measurement can then be applied. As was seen earlier, the participants in such reviews need real clarity regarding the behaviours expected of them. Open, constructive and supportive challenge is a vital part of these reviews. Such testing will determine the extent to which the required outputs have been attained and whether the processes, thinking and analysis behind them have been properly applied. This approach calls for organizational and facilitative skills, which are not always given sufficient emphasis in the selection of process sponsors. However, if the goal is to achieve stable, sustainable processes, producing predictable outputs, then this becomes a core capability.

Using baselining and benchmarking

To benchmark a company is to measure its performance against others. This allows the identification of its strengths and weaknesses, and an assessment of its relative position in terms of supply chain competence and capability. This is a different approach from baselining, which encourages an assessment of the full gap between current position and the totality of what can be achieved. The two methodologies are most effective when integrated together, as can be seen in Figures 11.7 and 11.8.

Step one is to identify the critical supply chain success factors. These will be the ones capable of providing sustainable business advantage. Map these factors for each separate stage of the supply chain and then group them according to their strategic development contribution (those that grow with the business and provide future

Figure 11.7

Benchmarking involves comparison against others. Baselining extrapolates into the future. You need to use both approaches

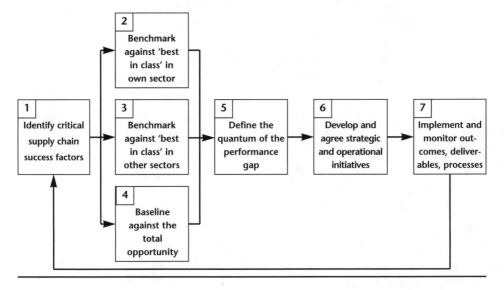

revenue streams) and operational improvement potential (those that will sustain and differentiate value delivery to customers).

Step two involves locating external benchmark companies within your own sector. Equally, you should be examining the best performing parts of your own company. These are the perceived leaders in strategic positioning and management of the supply chain. Ensure that you select not only your major competitors but also the emerging competitors who may present a significant competitive threat in the future.

However, do not concentrate only on companies from within your own sector. Step three requires an evaluation of the best in class leaders from other sectors. These will be the companies widely acknowledged as being excellent in a particular business discipline. You may wish to focus on a company and its entire interlinked business processes, or target on specific strands of the supply chain, such as purchasing, joint venturing, demand management or value

Figure 11.8

Benchmarking involves comparison against the current interpretation of best in class. Baselining extrapolates into the future

Cost Management. **Statement of Best Practice:** *At ease with the concept of year on year price reduction with a fully developed, sound price management programme. Suppliers will have been conditioned to seek and offer cost improvements. Within the business there is active support from all functions.*

	Weak	Basic	Proficient	Advanced	Expert
Cost Measurement	Cost performance is not measured.	Cost performance is measured via the business budget process (e.g. variances against annually agreed standard).	The principles of zero based measurement are understood and used to provide monthly results.	Zero based measurement is used to review cost performance, establish annual buyer targets and publicize results across the business.	Zero based measurement is a part of a comprehensive purchasing performance measurement system which covers all external expenditure.
Reporting Cost Performance	There is no evidence of reporting of cost management performance.	Report on past performance (zero based measurement) is issued frequently and regularly to senior managers.	Monthly purchasing report is issued to business managers. Focus is on future cost opportunity and risk.	Monthly purchasing report is issued to business managers. Focus is on future cost opportunity and risk. Performance is reviewed regularly at board meetings.	Monthly purchasing report is issued to business managers. Focus is on future cost opportunity and risk. Performance is reviewed monthly at board meetings.

© ADR International Purchasing Consultants.

delivery to customers, and then identify the leaders in these particular areas. Draw on public domain information from analysts' reports, market research bodies, trade press, general articles and items on the internet. Attend conferences. Form, and participate in, benchmarking clubs. The freely available information is often overwhelming. But, of course, it is equally available to everyone else. As such, and almost by definition, it is therefore most unlikely to provide benchmarkers with sources of competitive advantage. It will, however, flag up areas of potentially significant neglect in your supply chain processes. You can then put in place the internal business initiatives to accelerate the required phase of 'catch-up'. But if you want to secure maximum gain from this approach, then make sure the focus of the 'best in class' trawl is not just on the output indicators of superior performance. Be determined to discover how the benchmark company addressed a specific strategic or operational issue. In particular, examine very closely the human resource, organizational and motivational problems that are always associated with the process of change.

Benchmarking against those companies which are widely regarded as being leaders in the supply chain, however, may mean that a high percentage of large global or pan-regional companies are selected as prime targets. This may work well for similarly sized businesses. It is unlikely to be the most appropriate route for companies that are considerably smaller, since the nature and complexity of their supply chain processes may well be very different. These companies are advised to focus on the medium sized players and, in particular, to draw on the detailed knowledge of trade associations, specialist consultancies, local educational and university centres, and the available networks such as those sponsored by local chambers of commerce. This is also an area where forming and participating in benchmarking clubs with similar sized companies can be of real value.

'I hate the tough words. But we are trying to apply internally the same principles of the free market economy that the company is subject to globally.' Hubertus von Grunberg, Chairman, Continental Tyre, on the use of performance benchmarking to challenge company culture.

Step four, baselining, is the final source of evaluative data. This methodology extrapolates supply chain processes into the future in terms of what can potentially be achieved. A company can then gauge itself against the full range of what can be attained, rather than only applying a comparative analysis based on what competing companies have already achieved.

The fifth step, using the data obtained from benchmarking and baselining, is to identify the precise quantum of strategic and operational improvement required across the many processes of the supply chain.

In the final two stages, steps six and seven, a prioritized set of business initiatives are carefully mapped out under the sponsorship of top management. Clearly, these may consist of either programmes of continuous improvement or more radical breakthrough change.

In Appendix 1 to this book, an audit tool has been provided to facilitate the design and implementation of such change programmes.

Definition of Terms

Total shareholder return (TSR): share price appreciation plus dividends. A measure of the theoretical capital growth assuming all dividends are reinvested.

Economic value added (EVA): net operating profit less a charge for capital employed (cost of capital x capital employed). It is a measure of how effectively an organization adds value. Positive EVAs indicate value added. Negative EVAs indicate value destroyed.

Market value added (MVA): share capital plus debt less equity loans and retained earnings. A measure of the value the market attaches to an organization.

Earnings per share (EPS): profit divided by total share capital in issue. A measure of the absolute earning power of each unit of ownership. In particular, it measures the dilution effects of increasing the share capital in issue.

Return on sales (ROS): profit expressed as a percentage of sales. An indication of how much value the organization or personal customers place on the goods or services provided in relation to the costs of their provision.

Return on capital employed (ROCE): profit expressed as a percentage of investment in the company.

Return on net assets (RONA): profit expressed as a percentage of investment by the company.

Measurement and baselining action checklist

Activities to launch straight away

1. Identify the major supply chain processes in your organization and the activities that comprise them.
2. Task functional teams to draw together the various measures of performance that are currently in use.
3. Challenge the relevance and added value of each one. Assess how they are used and the extent to which they drive business, operational or individual improvement.
4. Review how effectively these measures are incorporated within executive meetings and other similar forums.
5. Benchmark your current supply chain processes against 'best in class' businesses elsewhere in your company and with competitors in similar sectors and elsewhere.

Initiatives to make a significant difference

1. Define the critical success factors for your organization in terms of supply chain positioning, market management and operational improvement.
2. Identify the crucial measures for these aspects of the supply chain. Co-ordinate an in-house baseline to gauge the performance gap.
3. Combine them into a coherent measurement framework, linking quantitative or financially orientated measures with the process underpinnings that sustain them. Ensure that these are focused on to future performance requirements.
4. Cascade strategic and operational measures down into the business. Deploy them within action planning workshops and strategic review forums.
5. Align individual objectives and team performance goals with business priorities. Structure remuneration schemes to reinforce required transformational changes.

CHAPTER TWELVE

Framing the agenda for action

Leveraging value across the supply chain

Never before have customers so quickly rewarded or so severely punished goods and service providers on the basis of value. The definition, creation, production, delivery and appropriation of value is an all-embracing framework for business today; it sets the agenda for action against which business development strategies, operational improvement initiatives and change management programmes across the complete supply chain are evaluated. Releasing value in business, and thereby meeting or exceeding the expectations of shareholders, owners, customers and other stakeholders, is the overarching goal of top executives. It drives:

'The correct definition of shareholder value is the pursuit of a long term strategy.' Klaus Liesen, Chairman of Ruhrgas and the Supervisory Board of Volkswagen.

- definition, location, control and protection of critical strategic capabilities;
- re-evaluation of markets, supply chains and product strategies;
- harnessing of knowledge and intellectual assets;
- innovative rather than imitative product development;
- rationalization of the supplier and manufacturing base;
- internal organizational alignment with such strategies.

Redefining the boundaries of business

The ongoing creation of a more homogeneous global economy, one in which 'comfortable and cosy' domestic markets disappear, is forcing companies to rethink and refocus on to their core business activities. Strategic outsourcing and deverticalization need serious attention.

Developing relational competence

'Chief executive officers are growing more convinced that leadership positions and dominant market shares are a prerequisite for enduring profitability.'
Jack Levy, Co-Head of Mergers & Acquisitions, Merrill Lynch.

There has been a rapid acceleration in the number of organizations building their expertise in closer, more synergistic relationships with suppliers and other third parties:

- cross-shareholdings and strategic alliances;
- joint ventures and licensing agreements;
- webs and networks of collaborating companies;
- technology exchanges and knowledge transfer;
- partnerships and similarly close supplier relationships;
- consortia and market alliances.

Success has been mixed. Frustration has sometimes been high. Understanding the appropriate circumstances under which firms with complementary capabilities decide to work together needs more searching consideration.

Managing at the right level

Despite the operational difficulties, competitive pressures are forcing many companies to rethink their businesses in global or transnational terms. Many consumer goods and service companies are promising annual growth of 10% plus in earnings per share. With the world's population growing at less than 2% per year on average, this means finding new international opportunities. This calls for:

- moving away from national markets as the defining basis for the organization of business activities;
- managing products, suppliers and processes at the most appropriate geographical level;
- strengthening cross-country co-ordination;
- preparing the supply base for global initiatives.

The responsive supply chain

Business strategies invariably fail as a result not of their design but of their execution. There is a real need for a strongly external orientation towards markets and customer needs. A wide array of initiatives have to be pursued:

- identifying and simplifying key supply chain processes;
- eliminating waste and non-value adding operations;
- designing products for manufacturability and logistics;
- rationalizing and consolidating the external supply base;
- minimizing stock holding and inventory reduction;
- shifting the emphasis from push supply to pull demand;
- streamlining warehousing and distribution;
- strengthening the information technology infrastructure to facilitate the flows of sales and stock data;
- reducing throughput and lead times;
- overcoming the functional divides and silos;
- developing capabilities and training the supply base.

Optimizing any one of these sub-processes is most unlikely to make a significant contribution to business performance. Equally, addressing individual activities within a single process, such as sourcing, has little impact. Transforming responsiveness needs an integrated approach.

Driving down purchase costs

External, bought-in purchases account for 60% of many businesses' total costs. A three pronged attack is recommended:

- price down, i.e. an aggressive attack on price through hit squads and project teams leveraging volume and consolidating expenditure;
- cost down, i.e. a more focused approach that shifts attention from the tactical initiatives of price down into more strategic management of the cost base;
- cost out, i.e. the adoption of joint development programmes by committed purchasers and their suppliers with full transparency on costs, open relationships and a principled approach to sharing the benefits.

'We used to be concerned about product performance: how the airplanes flew. While that's still important, we now have to look more at how much they cost.'
Frank Shrontz, Chairman of Boeing.

Bringing about change: strategic development vs. operational improvement

Organizations are being forced to rethink their business development strategies, in order to deal with rapid technological, commercial and social change. Radical adjustments in focus, positioning, product or service development and relational links with trading partners are required to keep the business on course and enable it to meet the ever greater demands of shareholders, owners, customers and other stakeholders. There are a number of critical success factors in effective change:

- developing strategic purpose through setting explicit goals and priorities across the supply chain;
- top management direction and active involvement in orchestrating the overall change programme;
- determining an appropriate strategy that balances the need for radical, business development led change with narrower operational process redesign (as can be seen in Figure 12.1);
- defining mission critical areas such as market management, redesign of supply chains, supplier responsive-

Figure 12.1

A range of strategies in supply chain change management needs to be evaluated and applied to meet specific business goals

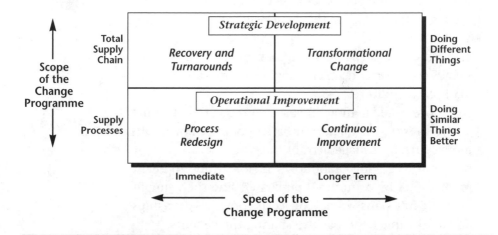

ness, product development and strategic target costing;

- cross-functional and cross-supply chain integration of effort and expertise to address these target areas;
- segmenting the various supply chains and supply processes and concentrating resources accordingly;
- strengthening the required change management capabilities such as project management and process measurement.

The electronic supply chain

Over the past ten years many businesses have adapted their operating processes to embrace the new technologies. A few have used them to locate additional routes to market. During the next decade this will accelerate. There will be a transformational shift forcing a re-evaluation of strategic fundamentals through:

'Mickey Mouse could do the cost cutting. It's much harder to know where to add and how to build.'
Al Dunlap, CEO, Sunbeam, on turnaround strategies and the location of new commercial opportunities.

- dematerialization, i.e. redeployment of supply chain assets;
- disintermediation, i.e. compression in the length of the supply chain;
- deverticalization, i.e. creation of extended enterprises linked with new electronic markets;
- data integration, i.e. real time access, capture and transfer of data between trading partners;
- development of new products, i.e. supporting and responding to electronic commerce.

The electronic supply chain needs urgent evaluation; in terms of its strategic business development potential and its role as a considerable enabler for operational redesign of many supply and demand processes.

Measurement and baselining

The need in performance measurement is to define how well a company has operated in the past but then, most crucially, determine what needs to be done in the future. This should remain the focus for top management attention. A key operating principle is that measurement should closely relate to individual and team accountability. If outputs from measurement are to be converted into action, it is essential that all relevant staff are actively involved. Ensure that the process can be translated into an approach that all employees can readily relate to during their day to day work. It is recommended that senior management:

- identify the key measurement areas, defined in relation to current and future strategic business development;
- combine them into a balanced and effective measurement framework that supports business development and operational improvement in terms of activity outcomes (the symptoms or indicators of effective performance) and the process drivers (the causative factors of successful supply chain performance);
- embed this system into the management culture by cascading the key measures down into the organization and linking them to business unit goals;
- align business, team and individual measurement with remuneration and similar human resources policies;
- develop and apply similar approaches with third party trading partners.

Monitoring of overall progress in the transformation of the supply chain can easily be achieved through profiling tools similar to the one illustrated in Figure 12.2.

Governance, ethics and supply sustainability

On occasions the choice between a company serving its stakeholders or its shareholders has been presented in somewhat stark terms. Successful executives realize that over the medium to longer term such a forced choice is inappropriate. The interests of both groups are increasingly aligned. This has been particularly true from the late 1980s and throughout the 1990s since awareness of environmental issues began to affect consumer shopping habits and product choice. The responsible corporation needs to pursue value added strategies in line with such consumer expectations. The corollary equally applies: that unethical and environmentally damaging practices can increase

Figure 12.2

Define the business priorities. Identify the supply chain initiatives. Map out the implementation plan. Measure the progress

Business Focus		Examples of Supply Chain Initiatives	Little Progress	Moving Forward	Fully Implemented
BUSINESS DEVELOPMENT STRATEGIES	Leveraging Value Across the Supply Chain	1. Segmentation of supply chains	●		
		2. Leveraging of intellectual assets		●	
		3. Strategies for volatile commodities		●	
	Redefining the Boundaries of Business	4. Strategic vs. secondary capabilities			●
		5. Deverticalization of the business		●	
		6. Innovation from suppliers	●		
	Developing Relational Competence	7. Profiling of relational types	●		
		8. Criteria definition and selection	●		
		9. Preferred suppliers and customers		●	
OPERATIONAL IMPROVEMENT STRATEGIES	Managing at the Right Level	10. Pan-regional consolidation		●	
		11. Sharing learning and best practice		●	
		12. Targeting intellectual services supply	●		
	The Responsive Supply Chain	13. Vendor managed inventory		●	
		14. Pull demand chain management		●	
		15. Integrated supply chain	●		
	Driving Down Purchase Costs	16. Analysis of total expenditure		●	
		17. Supplier involvement in design		●	
		18. Application of target costing	●		
CHANGE MANAGEMENT STRATEGIES	Bringing About Change	19. Supply chain strategic forum		●	
		20. Defined options in change	●		
		21. Use of bottom up quick wins		●	
	The Electronic Supply Chain	22. Development of new products	●		
		23. Application of ECR	●		
		24. Electronic transactional transfers		●	
	Governance, Ethics and Supply Sustainability	25. Appointment of board level sponsor			●
		26. Ethical and environmental standards		●	
		27. Full compliance with standards	●		
	Measurement and Baselining	28. Total corporate performance review	●		
		29. Quarterly reporting of progress		●	
		30. Defined baseline for innovation	●		

Typical supply chain profile of a medium sized company

business vulnerability and potentially undermine share-holder value.

'Pollution equals inefficiency. It is no longer enough simply to have resources. Using resources productively is what makes for competitiveness today.' Michael E. Porter and Claas Van Der Linde.

Furthermore, loss of name and corporate reputation through adverse publicity or disrupted supply can be business threatening and wreak havoc on brand or stock value. Companies need to pay real attention to how they are rated by customers. If only from an instrumental perspective, reputation has become a critical asset. It needs to be managed and safeguarded accordingly. Unfortunately, too many companies are ill prepared to rally to the defence of their reputation if it comes under challenge.

So it seems increasingly likely, therefore, that even those companies that are not instinctively minded to address ethical issues may find that a number of the following approaches will become increasingly difficult to ignore:

- setting environmental, social and ethical performance indicators;
- framing ethical policies that define acceptable and unacceptable commercial behaviour towards competitors, suppliers and customers;
- conducting a social and ethical audit of employment practice across the supply chain;
- revamping design and development processes to build environmental sustainability into products;
- reducing environmental impact through lean and customer responsive production methods;
- coaching, educating and communicating an appropriate ethical stance to employees.

However, each of the themes examined in this final chapter is provided only as a guide to action. It is not suggested that they be applied in a slavish or prescriptive fashion. Moreover, organizations need to redefine them within the context of their own specific business and cultural features. It is hoped that the following Appendix provides a systematic framework within which you can determine and prioritize the necessary supply chain interventions. The authors of this book wish you well in their application.

Auditing the supply chain

Instructions for completion of the audit tool:

Ten themes in transforming the supply chain have been included within the audit tool. They correspond with the core chapters of this book.

For each theme, you will find ten 'levers of change'. Please assess the priority of each one in the context of your business and organizational goals. Then assess the current and required level of progress that is necessary across the supply chain to secure sustainable competitive advantage.

Areas for strategic business development and supply chain improvement:

(1) Leveraging value across the supply chain

(2) Redefining the boundaries of business

(3) Developing relational competence

(4) Managing at the right level

(5) The responsive supply chain

(6) Driving down purchase costs

(7) Bringing about change

(8) The electronic supply chain

(9) Governance, ethics and supply sustainability

(10) Measurement and baselining

Support on the completion of the audit tool can be provided by contacting:

The Windsor Foundation for Business Development,
3, Cell Farm House, Church Road, Old Windsor,
Berkshire, SL4 2PG, UK.
Tel. 01753-622527. Fax 01753-622528.
Web: www.windsorfoundation.com

ADR North America LLC,
24 Frank Lloyd Wright Drive, Lobby C, PO Box 366,
Ann Arbor, Michigan 48106-0366, USA.
Tel. 734-930-5070. Fax 734-930-5080.
E-mail: adrna@ic.net

Theme No. 1: Leveraging value across the supply chain

Strategic business practice in the supply chain is about contributing substantially to profitability; acquiring, controlling and releasing appropriate value to customers; and maximizing returns to shareholders. This calls for active management of supply chains and markets.

Levers of change	Business Priority			Little Progress	Moving Forward	Fully Implemented
	Low	Moderate	High			
1.1 Clarity on required target returns and goals for shareholder value.	A	B	C	1	2	3
1.2 Definition of markets, supply chains and product strategies to achieve these goals.	A	B	C	1	2	3
1.3 Location, control and protection of critical strategic capabilities.	A	B	C	1	2	3
1.4 Definition and leveraging of intangible, intellectual and knowledge based assets.	A	B	C	1	2	3
1.5 Executive focus on to innovative rather than imitative product and service development.	A	B	C	1	2	3
1.6 Repositioning from commodities into product and service streams with high differentiation.	A	B	C	1	2	3
1.7 Segmentation of supply chains by strategic, operational and executional impact.	A	B	C	1	2	3
1.8 Active management of the supply chain to deliver superior product performance.	A	B	C	1	2	3
1.9 Development of strategies to impact volatile commodity markets.	A	B	C	1	2	3
1.10 Integration of market strategies into a plan of business development and renewal.	A	B	C	1	2	3

Executive audit:

Q1: What are the target returns to shareholders, and the implications of achieving them?

Q2: In which markets can a pre-eminent position be secured that commands premium prices?

Q3: Which business competencies and strategic capabilities need to be leveraged to achieve this?

Q4: How is maximum value captured and appropriated within supply chains?

Business summary:

Theme No. 2: Redefining the boundaries of business

The traditional boundaries of business are being blown apart. Accelerating competition, aggressive new entrants, deregulation and heightened pressures for capital productivity are forcing companies to redefine the way they operate.

Levers of change	Business Priority			Little Progress	Moving Forward	Fully Implemented
	Low	Moderate	High			
2.1 Definition of strategic and secondary operations and capabilities.	A	B	C	1	2	3
2.2 Evaluation of the balance between in-house control vs. deverticalization.	A	B	C	1	2	3
2.3 Location and evaluation of the prime targets for strategic and tactical outsourcing.	A	B	C	1	2	3
2.4 Development of the forward strategy for access to capabilities via strategic alliances.	A	B	C	1	2	3
2.5 Business realignment to accommodate institutional and sourced alliances.	A	B	C	1	2	3
2.6 Application of arm's length, modular, networked and virtual supply.	A	B	C	1	2	3
2.7 Transfer of control of major business processes to third parties.	A	B	C	1	2	3
2.8 Application of defined and standardized processes for post-merger integration.	A	B	C	1	2	3
2.9 Strengthening of supplier development capabilities and high order contractual skills.	A	B	C	1	2	3
2.10 Building management understanding of the implications of new ways of working.	A	B	C	1	2	3

Executive audit:

Q1: How will market competition, emerging technologies and new channels impact the business?

Q2: How will this drive consolidation, collaboration and co-operation between previous competitors?

Q3: Where do deverticalization of the business and strategic outsourcing need to be considered?

Q4: What ground rules, principles and operating practices are required to define the way forward?

Business summary:

Theme No. 3: Developing relational competence

A wide array of relational strategies are now being deployed across the supply chain. They embrace both collaborative and competitive forms of trading. The key is to develop appropriate criteria for the selection of these different types of trading relationships.

Levers of change	Business Priority			Little Progress	Moving Forward	Fully Implemented
	Low	Moderate	High			
3.1 Develop a clear business understanding of the full range of relational types.	A	B	C	1	2	3
3.2 Map different trading relationships to different business needs.	A	B	C	1	2	3
3.3 Profile the key factors in specific relationships with different suppliers.	A	B	C	1	2	3
3.4 Structure the selection criteria for the application of business relationships.	A	B	C	1	2	3
3.5 Align relational types to strategic and secondary capabilities.	A	B	C	1	2	3
3.6 Recognize the role of power and dependency within supply chains and relationships.	A	B	C	1	2	3
3.7 Develop preferred supplier and preferred customer approaches.	A	B	C	1	2	3
3.8 Assess the contribution of early supplier involvement in a range of business practices.	A	B	C	1	2	3
3.9 Use relational skill to capture and deploy innovation ahead of competitors.	A	B	C	1	2	3
3.10 Provide training, coaching and action learning in strategic negotiation.	A	B	C	1	2	3

Executive audit:

Q1: What range of relational strategies are available from acquisition through to the spot market?

Q2: What business criteria need to be applied to evaluate the appropriateness of relationships?

Q3: Where should executive resource be applied to derive the greatest business benefits?

Q4: What risks are associated with different relationships, and how can they be minimized?

Business summary:

Theme No. 4: Managing at the right level

Within medium to large businesses, determining the right level for control, ownership and delivery of supply chain processes raises important organizational issues. Balancing local autonomy with cross-business leverage of total resources needs close executive scrutiny.

Levers of change	Business Priority			Little Progress	Moving Forward	Fully Implemented
	Low	Moderate	High			
4.1 Assessing the appropriate level of geographical aggregation for supply chain processes.	A	B	C	1	2	3
4.2 Top level executive forum to assign process management to designated process sponsors.	A	B	C	1	2	3
4.3 Identification of local, country, regional and global supply chain processes.	A	B	C	1	2	3
4.4 Definition of appropriate levels of dependency on the local supply network.	A	B	C	1	2	3
4.5 Dealing with the inefficiencies of decentralization and capturing the synergies.	A	B	C	1	2	3
4.6 Pan-regional and global consolidation of purchasing to maximize supplier leverage.	A	B	C	1	2	3
4.7 Organization of networking events and away days to foster close working relationships.	A	B	C	1	2	3
4.8 Targeting the non-production and intellectual services supply chain for close scrutiny.	A	B	C	1	2	3
4.9 Defining guidelines and policies in cross business collaboration and training staff in them.	A	B	C	1	2	3
4.10 Sharing learning and best practice in pan-regional ways of working.	A	B	C	1	2	3

Executive audit:

Q1: What is the balance between decentralization, freedom to act and standardization?

Q2: What local or country business issues inhibit effective collaboration and consolidation?

Q3: Is there a formal business structure in place to capture the cross-business synergies?

Q4: How will the points of resistance within this structure be addressed?

Business summary:

Theme No. 5: The responsive supply chain

There is an accelerating trend towards greater integration of supply chains in terms of demand and supply management. This calls for radical reform of forecasting, planning, manufacturing, supplier management and inventory systems.

Levers of change	Business Priority			Little Progress	Moving Forward	Fully Implemented
	Low	Moderate	High			
5.1 Assess best practice on previous platforms of manufacturing and supply chain operations.	A	B	C	1	2	3
5.2 Determine short-term goals for inventory reduction.	A	B	C	1	2	3
5.3 Locate pilot projects for greater involvement of suppliers in new product development.	A	B	C	1	2	3
5.4 Negotiate agreements with retailers and other customers on two-way sharing of data.	A	B	C	1	2	3
5.5 Centralize distribution centres and develop the methodology of cross-docking.	A	B	C	1	2	3
5.6 Harness quantitative modelling techniques to provide more accurate and stable forecasts.	A	B	C	1	2	3
5.7 Abandon complex matrix structures and reduce hierarchical ways of working.	A	B	C	1	2	3
5.8 Replace sequential new product development with concurrent and integrated methods.	A	B	C	1	2	3
5.9 Redesign business processes around a pull system of demand management.	A	B	C	1	2	3
5.10 Rationalize suppliers and develop joint programmes of training and development.	A	B	C	1	2	3

Executive audit:

Q1: What are the true costs of inventory accumulation and time across the supply chain?

Q2: What would be the full impact on capital productivity of restructuring current processes?

Q3: What are the top priorities across inbound supply, internal production and customer delivery?

Q4: How should the internal points of resistance and functional barriers be addressed?

Business summary:

Theme No. 6: Driving down purchase costs

The purchased content of goods and services is well over 60% of total business costs in many sectors. Substantial savings can be made through tactical and strategic cost management. The goal is to secure, as a minimum, a cost advantage over direct competitors.

Levers of change	Business Priority			Little Progress	Moving Forward	Fully Implemented
	Low	Moderate	High			
6.1 Build a thorough understanding of the cost drivers within the purchase supply chain.	A	B	C	1	2	3
6.2 Analyse the total expenditure across production and non-production categories.	A	B	C	1	2	3
6.3 Rationalize the supply base and introduce robust supplier measurement.	A	B	C	1	2	3
6.4 Address in-company preferences, local ties and unjustifiable supplier dependencies.	A	B	C	1	2	3
6.5 Put cost reduction and cost containment plans in place and measure them regularly.	A	B	C	1	2	3
6.6 Use target costing to connect required product profitability with sourcing practice.	A	B	C	1	2	3
6.7 Brief suppliers and actively involve them in the target costing process.	A	B	C	1	2	3
6.8 Secure the support of suppliers for the practice of ongoing cost improvement.	A	B	C	1	2	3
6.9 Reduce total value of working assets through cash and inventory management.	A	B	C	1	2	3
6.10 Make the business cash positive, i.e. customer receipts ahead of supplier creditor terms.	A	B	C	1	2	3

Executive audit:

Q1: What actions are needed to reduce purchase costs by at least 25%?

Q2: How can that be done without eroding business performance elsewhere in the supply chain?

Q3: What are the major price down–cost down–cost out initiatives to pursue?

Q4: What does this mean in terms of the most appropriate way of integrating functions?

Business summary:

Theme No. 7: Bringing about change
There are a number of clear options available in change management. Required supply chain initiatives need to be designed within the context of the demands for change and the levels of internal support necessary to sustain it.

Levers of change	Business Priority			Little Progress	Moving Forward	Fully Imple-mented
	Low	Moderate	High			
7.1 Definition of a limited number of business mission critical supply chain processes.	A	B	C	1	2	3
7.2 Creation of a supply chain change manage-ment programme over a 1:3 year period.	A	B	C	1	2	3
7.3 Formation of a top level steering group with a vision of strategic supply chain excellence.	A	B	C	1	2	3
7.4 Cross-business collegiate support for the top business priorities in the supply chain.	A	B	C	1	2	3
7.5 Options in change management have been fully assessed and priorities determined.	A	B	C	1	2	3
7.6 Resourcing the business with talented staff capable of adding value in the supply chain.	A	B	C	1	2	3
7.7 Senior management determination to break down the functional silos and blocking forces.	A	B	C	1	2	3
7.8 Bottom up 'quick wins' change programme under way to build momentum.	A	B	C	1	2	3
7.9 Shake up the power structure inside the business. Destabilize the status quo.	A	B	C	1	2	3
7.10 Redefine, restructure and redesign the core supply chain processes.	A	B	C	1	2	3

Executive audit:

Q1: What type of supply chain change management programme is required?

Q2: Who should sponsor it, and be involved in its implementation?

Q3: What balance should be sought between consensus and imposition of change?

Q4: What are the gaps in individual and team competence and how will they be closed?

Business summary:

Theme No. 8: The electronic supply chain

The electronic supply chain is less about the available technology than it is about connectivity, new commercial behaviour and business development opportunities. Focus less on the technologies than on the ways in which they will impact on competitiveness.

Levers of change	Business Priority			Little Progress	Moving Forward	Fully Implemented
	Low	Moderate	High			
8.1 Evaluation of the ways in which markets may be created via electronic commerce.	A	B	C	1	2	3
8.2 Assessment of the scope for reduction, removal or redeployment of marketing assets.	A	B	C	1	2	3
8.3 Compression in the length of the supply chain through the elimination of stages.	A	B	C	1	2	3
8.4 Deverticalization of business via electronically linked extended enterprises.	A	B	C	1	2	3
8.5 Real time access, capture and transfer of data between trading partners.	A	B	C	1	2	3
8.6 Development of new products and services which support electronic commerce.	A	B	C	1	2	3
8.7 Access to pan-regional and global markets for the supply of goods and services.	A	B	C	1	2	3
8.8 Application of efficient consumer response between linked trading partners.	A	B	C	1	2	3
8.9 Conversion of the supply chain from a push to a pull demand chain.	A	B	C	1	2	3
8.10 Support for low value commodity purchasing and electronic transactional transfers.	A	B	C	1	2	3

Executive audit:

Q1: What is the business vision of the full potential of electronic trading?

Q2: How will it create, adapt or replace defined markets for goods and services?

Q3: What risks and vulnerabilities may be encountered, and how should they be minimized?

Q4: What technology enablers need to be evaluated and piloted across the business?

Business summary:

Theme No. 9: Governance, ethics and supply sustainability

There are ambiguities, risks and rewards in adopting an explicitly ethical stance to business. The responsible corporate citizen should pursue value added strategies in line with customer and consumer expectations. Unacceptable business practice can damage long-term earnings.

Levers of change	Business Priority			Little Progress	Moving Forward	Fully Implemented
	Low	Moderate	High			
9.1 Appointment of a board level sponsor with accountability for commercial values and ethics.	A	B	C	1	2	3
9.2 Produce a values statement and ethical framework on acceptable business practices.	A	B	C	1	2	3
9.3 Set up task groups to examine particularly sensitive areas.	A	B	C	1	2	3
9.4 Publicize ethical and environmental statements to shareholders and trade bodies.	A	B	C	1	2	3
9.5 Conduct an annual independent audit of commercial and environmental integrity.	A	B	C	1	2	3
9.6 Incorporate findings within internal training programmes and with suppliers.	A	B	C	1	2	3
9.7 Develop appropriate monitoring practices to ensure compliance with ethical policies.	A	B	C	1	2	3
9.8 Develop strategies for dealing with cartels, collusion, market fixing and corruption.	A	B	C	1	2	3
9.9 Join forces in trade consortia to apply pressure for liberalization of trade.	A	B	C	1	2	3
9.10 Incorporate ethical and environmental standards within sourcing strategies.	A	B	C	1	2	3

Executive audit:

Q1: What are deemed to be ethical and unethical business practices in a specific sector?

Q2: What is the company's position going to be with regard to indefensible commercial practice?

Q3: How can risks and vulnerabilities associated with negative customer reaction be minimized?

Q4: What are the Board accountabilities for appropriate trading values and standards?

Business summary:

Theme No. 10: Measurement and baselining

Measurement has a pivotal role in transformational supply chain change. It builds commitment, motivates teams and generates forward momentum. An effective measurement scheme needs to be embedded within the business culture and regularly reviewed by top management.

Levers of change	Business Priority			Little Progress	Moving Forward	Fully Implemented
	Low	Moderate	High			
10.1 Integrating supply chain measurement within total corporate performance reviews.	A	B	C	1	2	3
10.2 Developing appropriate measures of inputs from suppliers.	A	B	C	1	2	3
10.3 Developing appropriate measures of 'value added' within the business.	A	B	C	1	2	3
10.4 Developing appropriate measures of process efficiency in task accomplishment.	A	B	C	1	2	3
10.5 Developing appropriate measures of outputs to customers.	A	B	C	1	2	3
10.6 Targeting improvement activity via quarterly reporting and regular review forums.	A	B	C	1	2	3
10.7 Linking supply chain metrics to staff performance management, e.g. MBO appraisals.	A	B	C	1	2	3
10.8 Creation of a forward looking baseline of required supply chain improvement.	A	B	C	1	2	3
10.9 Creation of a supply chain strategy forum involving top management.	A	B	C	1	2	3
10.10 Independent audit of results of supply chain strategies and improvement activities.	A	B	C	1	2	3

Executive audit:

Q1: How do supply chain deliverables impact shareholder value and earnings per share?

Q2: How can these deliverables be measured effectively?

Q3: What process is required to assess and review supply chain performance?

Q4: How will the causative factors of performance be monitored by executive management?

Business summary:

Strategic Linkage and Supply Chain Initiatives		
Priority Business Needs	*Priority Supply Chain Initiatives*	*Immediate Actions*

Summary of Forward Action Plan		
Executive Sponsors	*Team Members to be Involved*	*Specific Actions*

Further reading

There are an increasing number of publications available which are relevant to those seeking to develop their understanding of the supply chain. The following books and articles are especially recommended.

Chapter one. Reversing neglect: Releasing the value

Bryan, L. and Farrell, D. (1996) *Market Unbound: Unleashing Global Capitalism*, John Wiley.

Treacy, M. and Wiersema, F. (1995) *The Discipline of Market Leaders: Choose Your Customers, Narrow Your Focus, Dominate Your Market*, Harper Collins.

Chapter two. Leveraging value across the supply chain

Brooking, A. (1996) *Intellectual Capital: Core Asset for the Third Millennium Enterprise*, International Thomson Business Press.

Cox, A. (1997) *Business Success: A Way of Thinking About Strategy, Critical Supply Chain Assets and Operational Best Practice*, Earlsgate Press.

Hamel, G. and Prahalad, C.K. (1994) *Competing for the Future*, Harvard Business School Press.

Kay, J. (1993) *Foundations of Corporate Success*, Oxford University Press.

Lamont, D. (1996) *Winning Worldwide – Strategies for Dominating Global Markets*, Capstone Publishing.

Porter, M.E. (1980) *Competitive Advantage: Creating and Sustaining Superior Performance*, Free Press.

Porter, M.E. (1985) *Competitive Strategy: Techniques for Analyzing Industries and Competitors*, Free Press.

Chapter three. Redefining the boundaries of business

Bowman, E.H., Singh, H., Useem, M. and Bhadury, R. (1997) *When Does Restructuring Work?* Wharton Business School, University of Pennsylvania.
EIS Report 320 (1996) *Outsourcing: A Flexible Option for the Future*, Institute of Employment Studies, University of Sussex.
Goold, M. and Luchs, K.S. (1996) *Managing the Multibusiness Company*, International Thomson Business Press.
Lewis, J.D. (1995) *The Connected Corporation: How Leading Companies Win Through Customer-Supplier Alliances*, Free Press.
Moore, J.F. (1996) *The Death of Competition: Leadership and Strategy in the Age of Business Ecosystems*, Harper Business.
Rothery, B., and Robertson, I. (1995) *The Truth About Outsourcing*, Gower.
White, R. and James, B. (1997) *The Outsourcing Manual*, Gower.

Chapter four. Developing relational competence

Brandenburger, A.M. and Nalebuff, B.J. (1996) *Co-opetition*, Currency Doubleday Business.
Cox, A. (1996) Relational Competence and Strategic Procurement Management: Towards an Entrepreneurial & Contractual Theory of the Firm, *European Journal of Purchasing and Supply Management*, 2(1), pp. 57-70.
Ralf, M., Hughes, E.J. and Cox, A. (1995) Developing Purchasing Leadership: Competing on Competence, *Purchasing & Supply Management*, October, pp. 37-42.
Yoshino, M.Y. and Rangan, U.S. (1995) *Strategic Alliances: An Entrepreneurial Approach to Globalization*, Harvard Business School Press.

Chapter five. Managing at the right level

Bartlett, C.A., Doz, Y. and Hedlund, G. (1990) *Managing the Global Firm*, Routledge.
Goold, M., Campbell, A. and Alexander, M. (1994) *Corporate Level Strategy: Creating Value in the Multibusiness Company*, John Wiley.
Kanter, R.M. (1996) *World Class: Thriving Locally in the Global Economy*, Simon & Schuster.
Maister, D.H. (1994) *Managing the Professional Service Firm*, Simon & Schuster.

Chapter six. The responsive supply chain

Harrison, B. (1994) *Lean and Mean: The Changing Landscape of Corporate Power in the Age of Flexibility*, Basic Books.

Hines, P. (1994) *Creating World Class Suppliers*, Financial Times and Pitman.

Lamming, R. (1993) *Beyond Partnership: Strategies for Innovation and Lean Supply*, Prentice Hall.

Rommel, G. *et al* (1997) *Quality Pays*, Macmillan Business.

Syrett, M. and Lammiman, J. (1997) *From Leanness to Fitness: The Role of HR in Developing Corporate Muscle*, IPD Publishing.

Womack, J.P., Jones, D.T. and Roos, D. (1996) *The Machine that Changed the World*, Rawson Associates.

Chapter seven. Driving down purchase costs

Case, J. (1997) Opening the Books, *Harvard Business Review* (March - April) pp. 118-127.

Jackson, R. and Evans, P. (1996) *The Purchasing Opportunity Performance Program*, NAPM 81st Annual International Purchasing Conference Proceedings.

Matthews, J. and Jackson, R. (1997) *Targeting Purchasing for Product Profitability*, NAPM 82nd Annual International Purchasing Conference Proceedings.

Chapter eight. Bringing about change

Beer, M., Eisenstat, R.A. and Spector, B. (1991) *The Critical Path to Corporate Renewal*, Harvard Business School Press.

Fry, J.N. and Killing, J.P. (1989) *Strategic Analysis and Action*, Prentice Hall.

Hammer, M. and Champy, J. (1993) *Re-engineering the Corporation: A Manifesto for Business Revolution*, Nicholas Brealey.

Hughes, E.J., Cox, A. and Ralf, M. (1995) Facilitating Strategic Change – The Key Role for Purchasing Leadership, *Purchasing & Supply Management*, November, pp. 44-48.

Pascale, R. (1990) *Managing on the Edge*, Viking Penguin.

Strebel, P. (1992) *Breakpoints: How Managers Exploit Radical Business Change*, Harvard Business School Press.

Chapter nine. The electronic supply chain

Cairncross, F. (1997) *The Death of Distance: How the Communications Revolution Will Change Our Lives*, Orion Business Books.

Emmelhainz, M.A. (1990) *Electronic Data Interchange: A Total Management Guide*, Van Noostrand Reinhold.

Mukhopadhyay, T., Kekre, S. and Kalathur, S. (1995) Business Value of Information Technology: A Study of EDI, *MIS Quarterly*, June, pp. 137-156.

Upton, D.M. and McAfee, A. (1996) The Real Virtual Factory, *Harvard Business Review*, 74(4), July/August, pp. 123-133.

Chapter ten. Governance, ethics and supply sustainability

Connock, S. and Johns, T. (1995) *Ethical Leadership*, IPD.

Fiorentini, G. and Peltzman, S. (1996) *The Economics of Organised Crime*, The Centre for Economic Policy Research, Cambridge University Press.

Fombrun, C.J. (1996) *Reputation – Realizing the Value from the Corporate Image*, Harvard Business School Press.

Institute of Grocery Distribution (1994) *Environmental Impact Management*, IGD.

Korten, D.C. (1995) *When Corporations Rule the World*, Kumarian Press & Berrett-Koehler Publishers.

Sternberg, E. (1994) *Just Business*, Little Brown.

Zohar, D. (1997) *Rewiring the Corporate Brain: Using the New Science to Rethink How We Structure and Lead Organizations*, Berrett-Koehler Publishers.

Chapter eleven. Measurement and baselining

Camp, R.C. (1989) *Benchmarking: The Search for Industry Best Practices That Lead to Superior Performance*, ASQC Quality Press.

Finnigan, J.P. (1996) *The Managers Guide to Bench-marking: Essential Skills for the Competitive Co-operative Economy*, Prentice Hall.

Karlof, B. and Ostblom, S. (1993) *Benchmarking: A Signpost to Excellence in Quality and Productivity*, John Wiley & Sons Ltd.

Lynch, R.L. and Cross, K.F. (1995) *Measure Up! How to Measure Corporate Performance*, 2nd Edition, Blackwell.

Norton, D. and Kaplan, R. (1995) *The Balanced Scorecard*, Harvard Business School Press.

Index